25 oo

N

shelf 15 50

EL

D1608811

Oriental Costume

DISCARDED

Oriental Costume

Jacqueline Ayer

UPSALA COLLEGE LIBRARY
WIRTHS CAMPUS

Charles Scribner's Sons · New York

With love for my mother and father

Copyright © 1974 Jacqueline Ayer

Copyright under the Berne Convention.

All rights reserved. No part of this book may be
reproduced in any form without the permission
of Charles Scribner's Sons.

First published in the UK by Studio Vista,
a division of Cassell and Collier Macmillan
Publishers Ltd.

1 3 5 7 9 11 13 15 17 19 I/C 20 18 16 14 12 10 8 6 4 2

Printed in Great Britain
Library of Congress Catalog Card Number 74-3771
ISBN 0-684-14024-1

Contents

Preface   7

The Heritage of the Past   9

The First Civilizations of the River Valleys   16

    The Indus   16

    The Yellow River   19

Basic Wraps and Cuts   24

The Courts   34

  The King: *The God King*   34

             The Son of Heaven   40

             The Earthly Counterpart   47

  The Courtiers: *The Indian Court*   49

                 The Celestial Courts of China   61

                 The Warrior Court of Japan   64

  The Inner Chamber   73

The Temple   79

  The Theatre: *Indian Theatre*   85

               Chinese Theatre   96

               Japanese Theatre   97

The Villages   102

  India: Landscape and People   102

  Out of the Past   127

  An Overall View   128

The Towns and Cities   138

Notes on the Plates   150

Some Common Terms   191

016872

Preface

On a strip of road crossing the desert between Delhi and Jaipur, from a car window I can see a trail of women walking to market. In the ageless frieze-like manner, they file singly with pots and bundles balanced on their heads. The women are in brutal contrast to the landscape that stretches flat, dry and vacant. The colours they wear are deep and rich, matt tones, brilliant against the parched land and white sky.

In my years of working and living in the East, when the sense of seeing is awakened like that moment in India, the idea of somehow collecting those moments and the sketches and scribbles that they inspire has for a long time been suggesting itself to my crowded schedule.

After the initial rush of impressions it is all too easy to walk through alien crowds, no longer really seeing and appreciating the differences. In my fifteen years in and out of the East, my interest and work in colour and fabric, drawing and fashion has given me the opportunities and open doors to areas and situations that have kept this awareness alert.

So, despite the immensity of the task, the impossibility of being able to say everything – the concept of oriental costume is hardly a straight and ordered road, but a complexity of forks and divergent paths – I have decided to make use of what I have seen and what I have come to know. For practical purposes I have limited my scope to finite and self-imposed borders. The better method of life-long endeavour seems to have disappeared along with the Victorians, who as dedicated amateurs had the luxury of a lifetime to devote.

What I have tried to portray are people in clothes, at work or in their natural stances caught unaware, and, more often than one would wish, standing stock still looking at me. I have also drawn upon the rich evidence of Art, that in unequalled ways has caught the essence of people in their ordinary and God-like images.

Through the distillation of my pen, if I have caught a portion of the richness and variety of what has been and what is now so threatened by an international set of modes and mores, and fixed it for the moment on a printed page, then that is what I've set out to do.

There is a fair amount of published reference to Asian costumes. The Japanese have a rich tradition of a costume culture. The Chinese also, though to a much lesser degree. India is verbosely documented, but so often with the bias of prudery or with a harsher failing – snobbery. There is hardly any overall view of Asian costume as an entity.

So much of oriental costume, when isolated in museum showcases either in folded and duly labelled piles, pinned flat on a wall surface, or displayed on unpliable dummies, misses the most important aspect: movement and body.

In rural India, the farm labourer climbing out of the fields or women at a village well say so much more for the wrapped garment than verbal listings or diagrams of the multiple ways of tying a dhoti or arranging a sari. The length of calf, the bony knee, the angular shoulders, the stretched gesture of the pot bearer, all the built-in angular or fluid movements of working people cannot be separated from the length of cloth. The garment is as natural to their working functions as the long muscles of the back. In the towns and cities and in the old feudal courts where life is more isolated from the simple and hardworking demands that were made of the body, dress is less purely efficient and is more the expression of other values. The sleek, tightly bound sari of the Air India hostess and the cumbersome sari of the city matron are more complex variations of the same ageless wrap.

In urban Thailand, ancient costume is relegated almost exclusively to a self-conscious attempt to keep up tradition by the upper classes. Uniforms in navy and white, khaki and white – blouses and skirts, shirts and trousers – and mass-produced international styles are much more in evidence. Only in the simpler trades of the boatsmen and market people is there any use of what might be termed a national costume and an indigenous working dress.

The political upheavals in China have given rise to an even more dedicated avoidance of individual dress. The uniform has attempted to cross the gaps and barriers of the old class system. In Japan, on the other hand, a deep-rooted sense of costume still prevails. Though urban Japan looks like any metropolitan development anywhere, through an intense awareness, which is particularly Japanese, in the love of detail and minutiae, their traditional dress is well documented and respected. In rural Japan, where the demands of city life are softened, and in the city, off the streets and in the recesses of private life, attempts to hold on to the older orders of another time succeed – with an ease and naturalness which seem to abate the relentlessness of the move towards conformity.

The Heritage of the Past

When one escapes from the crowds and traffic of Asian cities, not far from the edges of pavement and high-rise buildings, it seems that history lies slumbering and undisturbed by the modern havoc. Follow a muddy stream on the outskirts of Bangkok, or go at right-angles into the fields off a commercial highway outside Delhi, or take a short train journey beyond Tokyo, and life seems stopped at a moment far in the past.

The consciousness of history and tradition has always till now given the Asian a sense of belonging, not only to his own family group, his clan and village but has also given to the individual a sense of his part in the stream of history. The survival of unbroken costume traditions over thousands of years within the present fibre of Asian rural life and religious practices has been the product of this sense of continuity. Roughly speaking, because of this unbroken strong line of traditions we can see deep in the past the emerging qualities

that have even five millenniums later survived as distinctive traits that set the costume cultures apart.

In the Indian culture, including her Buddhist and Hindu colonies to the south-east, the idealized human form takes heroic and voluptuous proportions. The body is hung and wrapped with ornaments, draped, but not to conceal, with fluid and fine fabrics. In essence – the decorated human form.

Throughout the immense but relatively uniform culture of China the body is more concealed. In fact the dominant aspect of the costume is not the wearer, as in the Indian sub-continent and South-East Asia, but the garment. The flowing robes or padded layers characteristic of the area denote the status of the wearer: rich and precious fabric for a ruler; awesome but austere splendour for a sage; a fierce aspect for a warrior. These distinctions are shown more obviously in the basic shape of the costume than in the detail of ornaments.

In Japan, the sense of dress is primarily architectural. With their heightened sense of aesthetics the Japanese almost ignore the basic body shape. A structure of high refinement uses the body only as a frame to layer shapes and forms. The early Haniwa figures of Japan, in very simple but with highly sculptural means, reflect this attitude. These figures are not individuals, but highly stylized aspects of the decorative standard.

The Chinese, who were equally powerful as conquerors and teachers, venerated the qualities of fierce strength and patient endurance. The former is exemplified by the Ming tomb guardian (p. 15, fig. h), layered in padded shields, at his waist a gargoyle to give weight to his massive strength, and the latter by the T'ang court ladies in their quiet length of drape, describing a passive and enduring stability.

The Mohenjo-daro figurine of pre-historic India, the Chieng San Buddha from fourteenth-century Thailand, though sculpted to express widely divergent ideals, define for our purposes the same aspect: the decorated nude.

a

b

c

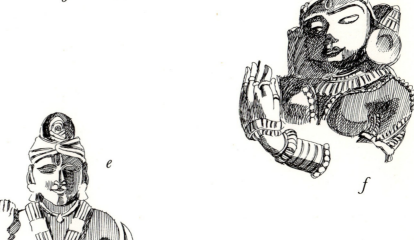

e

f

d

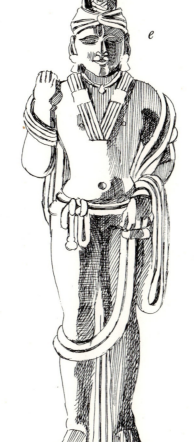

g

a

b

c

d

e

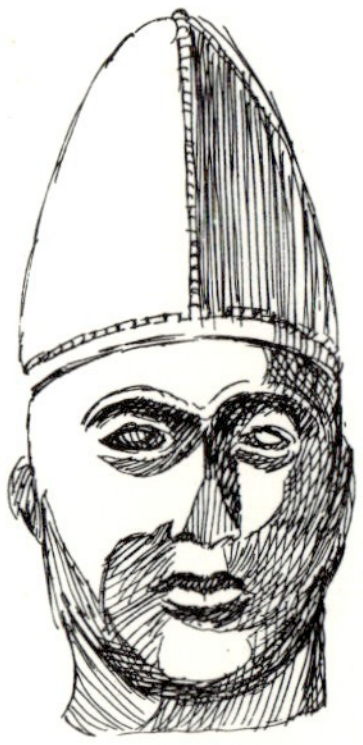

f

g

h

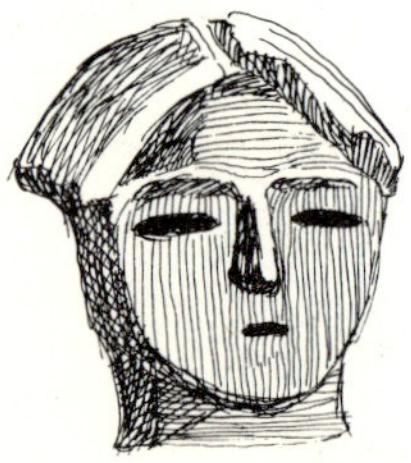

i

j

k

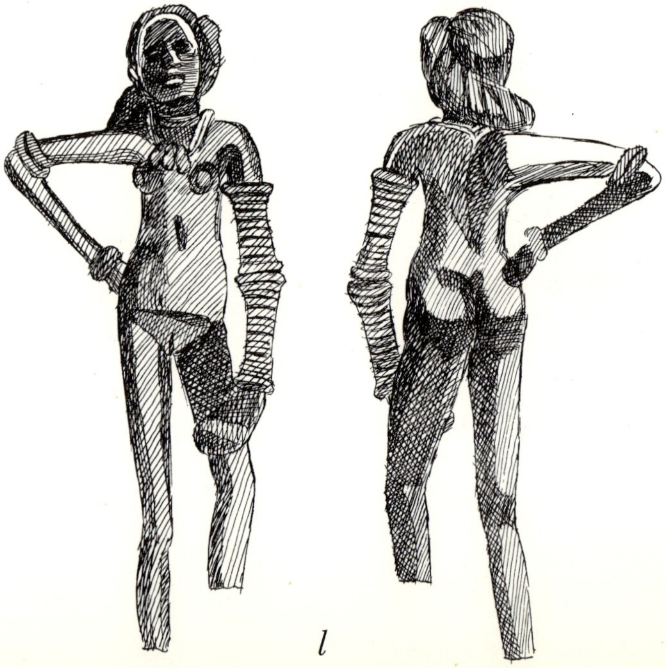

l

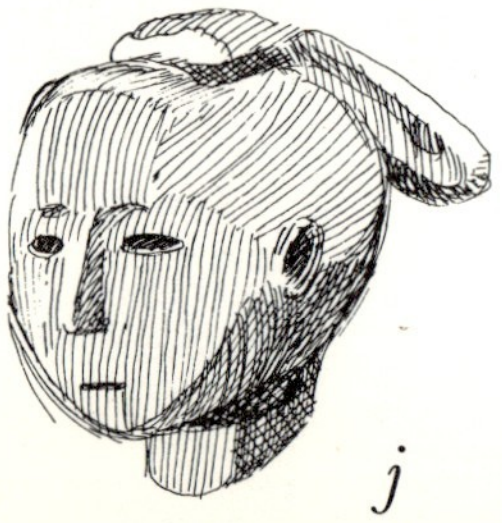

12

a

b

c

d

e

f

g

h

i

j

13

a

b

c

d

e

f

g

h

i

14

a

b

c

d

e

f

g

h

The First Civilizations
of the River Valleys

The Indus

The first three great civilizations grew to strength in the fertile river valleys of the Nile, the Indus and the Yellow River. As isolated awakened giants they separately developed the skills of civilized culture.

Along the Nile River valley about 2800 BC the Old Kingdom of Egypt solidified out of a group of feuding tribes and villages. As the water and land routes were not yet accessible, Egypt thrived in safety.

Concurrently, village tribes from what is now Pakistan migrated south to the moist Indus valley and ultimately unified in agricultural communities in Baluchistan. The cities along the Indus, notably Mohenjo-daro on the lower Indus and Harappa 400 miles to the north-east, were prosperous priest-king states. Their highly organized system of government differed sharply from the neighbouring village cultures.

So uniform was the pattern of the Indus civilization that streets were planned to a consistent scheme, a strict system of weights and measures was developed, and even bricks were of a standardized size and shape. With a thriving agricultural economy, the Indus valley civilization attained a rigid and conservative culture, if a rather unimaginative one. The quality of life was comfortable for the bourgeoisie, and even the labouring class, although they were bondsmen or slaves, had the comparative luxury of two-room brick cottages. Commerce with neighbouring village cultures as well as trade in precious metals and stones from further Persia and Afghanistan, and jade from Central Asia, supported a stable regime. Resting on the consolidated strengths of a strong centralized government and fortified power, this civilization survived centuries without threat. With the luxury of time and safety, the basic aspects of Indian culture and life developed. Cotton was first used by the Harappa people. Wild rice was cultivated, and water buffalo and small fowl were tamed.

In the early part of the second millenium BC the migratory

Aryans spread from Iran and south-east Europe. They brought with them the worship of sky gods and their horses and chariots. The peaceful and stagnant cities of the Indus could neither withstand nor absorb the invaders, and they collapsed and were abandoned. With the coming of the Aryans and the conquest of the Indus valley in 1550 BC a new and more volatile culture unfolded.

At this point in time Indian written history begins. The development of the Upanishad scriptures in 700 BC was to set the tone for all further religious thought in India. Courtly theatre as well as popular folk drama depicting the mythology of gods and demons, from which Sanskrit drama was to evolve, was developed. Trade and intermittent skirmishes with the cultures of Greece and middle Europe made for a constantly changing and growing civilization. The daily life and routine of the villages and cities of Vedic times was to reflect these influences. Everyday village life was not unlike present-day rural India.

The garments worn as early as 3000 BC are prototypes for those still found in hill and plain throughout the Indian continent and sub-cultures to the south and east. Basically the garments were wrapped and tied lengths of cloth. Unstitched lengths were wrapped around the hips and draped over the shoulders. The hip wrap was either tied or fastened around the waist with a belt or string. An upper shawl was hung or draped over the shoulders. A third length of greater proportions was also draped like a cloak in the colder climates.

The only difference between the sexes in garments was in the size and pattern of the cloth and in the manner of draping or tying. The women were bare-breasted but wore ornate necklaces and loops of flowers.

Differences in status were expressed in the width, length and quality of fabric but the basic garment was the same for all classes. In the lower orders the hip wrap was no more than a loincloth or a short skirt. The wealthy and the royal wore long ankle-length wraps, often pleated in decorative folds at the front and held in place with jewelled girdles. Sometimes the end of the cloth was twisted and pulled through the legs and tucked at the back – the kanch tuck (dhoti). This method varied in style from limb-fitting trouser in a fine silk muslin carefully draped, to a haphazard arrangement in rough cotton of the farmer. Or alternatively the end of a long cloth would be thrown over the shoulders as a continuation of the hip wrap in the style of a Roman toga or the present-day sari.

Stitched garments were used as well but to a lesser degree. Women are often portrayed wearing short bodices or jackets and in the north trousers and shirts were common. The horse cultures from central Asia introduced long quilted coats and trousers and stitched or wrapped boots.

Garments were simple and limited in style, but ornaments and body decoration were complex. Jewellery was used in every possible area. For women at the parting of the hair, the edge of the ear, on their faces and foreheads. (Nose rings, however, did not appear until after the Muslim conquest.) Necks were constricted with layers of circlets, ears were distended with rings and jewelled plugs. Both men and women wore earrings and plugs, and as well loops of gold and jewelled necklaces, bracelets, anklets and lengths of jewelled ropes across the chest and over the hips.

The simple people made do with ornaments of brass, glass and painted pottery; and all classes decorated their hair, ears and necks with fragrant flowers.

Use of sandalwood and kohl as cosmetics and for decorative body painting was made by both sexes. Also, women dyed their lips, the tips of toes and fingers, and their palms and soles with red lac.

The Yellow River

Civilization in the Far East rose in the midst of a barbarous and ungenerous land. The hazards of keeping alive were much greater than in the humid fertile valleys of the Nile or Indus. In 1700 BC amongst primitive Stone Age villages in the rich Yellow River basin the Shang created a culture as rich and refined as the Egyptians'. From a neolithic culture, the Shang mysteriously developed the skills and luxuries of a high civilization. They introduced a complex system of writing and the crafts of working bronze, marble, jade and ivory, and they discovered silk and developed fine weaving. From earlier tribal religions the Shang evolved the beginnings of a sophisticated religious philosophy of ancestor worship.

The Shang were robust warriors and hunters. They lived intensely, taking pleasure or death with equal vigour. Feared by their enemies as 'the great terror of the East' they tamed the harsh realities of proto-historic China. As warriors, they were highly organized and mounted armies of 30,000. Almost constantly at war, the Shang fortunately enjoyed it for the sport as well as for victory.

Their warrior nobility, both men and women, wore furs over fine silks – silk gowns that were stitched and cross-closed, waisted with tied broad sashes. The robes were often worn one layered over others, or padded with silk floss. The Shang were dedicated horsemen and the padded trousers and sturdily constructed boots were considered by the gentler valley people of the Indus as the mark of the barbarian. Jewellery of bone, shell and jade was finely fashioned and both sexes wore elaborate hair arrangements which were skewered with long ivory and bone pins.

Despite their boisterous and warlike qualities, the Shang pursued more peaceful endeavours as well with equal energy. The workmanship of their bronze carvings places them amongst the finest of any civilization; the art of music was sophisticated; and modern Chinese writing is directly descended from the Shang style.

Although the Shang dynasty fell in the eleventh century BC to the less gifted Chou, their heritage is still marked in modern China. The Chou in turn some eight centuries later were conquered by the Ch'in, in 221 BC. It was at this time that the Great Wall of China was built, typifying the vast civilization established under the Ch'in. Medieval China stretched as a unified empire from Inner Mongolia to Vietnam, from Tibet to Japan. The spread of the rice-growing culture and dedication to the land, the embracing philosophy of the ancestor cult, and Confucian ethics were to extend its influence, most importantly to Korea, Japan and Vietnam. Though Japan and Korea were dominated both politically and culturally for a thousand years, gradually they developed their separate but still very related cultures.

Japan, China

a

b

a

b

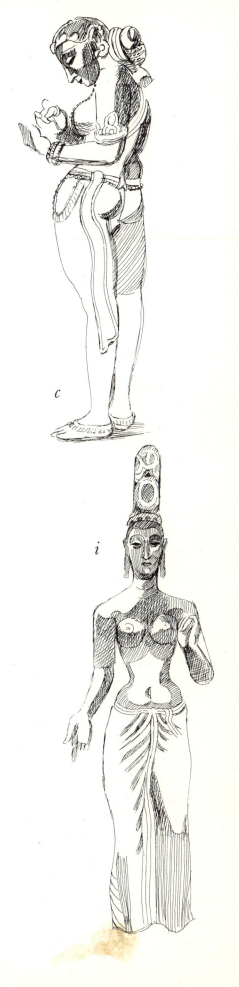

c

i

d

e

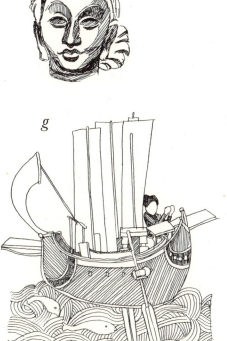

g

h

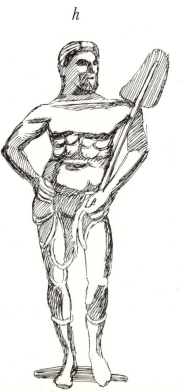

f

Basic Wrap and Cuts

Spanning the millenniums and the stretch of Asia, certain basic wraps and cuts appear. Despite the embellishments and the particular demands of use and climate one can trace fundamental forms, which underlie and give cohesion to the wealth of variations. These basic forms are especially noticeable as the volatility of European fashion is not found in Oriental dress.

Reduced to its simplest form the draped unsewn garment consists of a rectangle of cloth. Its length varies but the width is dictated by ultimate use or, as often as not, by the capabilities of the loom.

As a short hip wrap or skirt, the cloth is wrapped tightly lengthwise over the hips then tied, tucked or secured with a belt at the waist. Because it is a simple and obvious use of cloth over the body this basic wrapped style is common in hot climates or simple cultures where the minimum covering is required.

When the width of the fabric is increased, the same wrap is worn full width as a long skirt, or at times somewhat narrower falling to knee length.

This simple hip wrap, long and short, is worn by both sexes. The female sarong or lunghi is usually wrapped to the left side and pulled sharply across the hips and stomach and tucked and tied with a belt or string. Sometimes the length is stitched to form a cylinder and folded, slipped and wrapped over the hips in the same manner. It can be worn pulled very tight almost to the point of restricting movement to mincing steps. Or at times more sedately as a rather straight and loosely hanging shaft. A contemporary Thai young woman might pull the length tightly across a minimal width of hip.

A Burmese matron of ampler proportions might ease the wrap. The same wrap was used as an underskirt by the Manchu upper class. The fabric was often of a delicate, elaborately embroidered silk. A plain cotton or sturdier silk band would be added to the width, and tied and rolled over at the waist to form a rather rigid unrevealing shape. This mode is also applicable to hill and tribal areas where the Chinese influence is marked or where dense woven fabrics require a more supple waist banding.

Men wear the long wrap skirt, particularly in south India, Thailand and Burma, in patterns and weaves reserved for male wear. The male lunghi is usually wrapped and crossed to the right, or wrapped and tied leaving the ends loose and rather free to the breezes. Constant retying and rewrapping is typical of this style. As simple as this wrap seems to be, it takes a manner of movement and a flat hipped body shape to wear it comfortably and successfully.

As another variant with cloth of more ample length, the fabric is centred at the back, wrapped over the hips and tied at the waist. The remaining length is gathered at the front waist, the tips brought together, twisted and looped between the legs and tucked at the small of the back. Using the narrow-width cloth or folding or crushing a wider width the resultant style is a very short loin-cloth leaving the legs free, and at times very abbreviated as only a waist band with a panel between the legs.

The traditional Indian dhoti is wrapped in this way, using a cloth of approximately a metre's width. The initial skirt wrap is well below the knee. When the ends are brought together and looped between the legs and tucked at the back, the resultant shape is, depending on the quality and character of the cloth and the care taken by the wearer, either loose and haphazard, fluid and wrapped neatly over the thighs, or starched crisp and standing away from the limbs. In a very rough homespun cotton, limp and loose, the dhoti tends to hang loosely in undisciplined folds, one 'leg' usually longer than the other. As a working costume, the application is of necessity casual and unaffected. The use of a finer quality of cloth calls for more careful and elaborate shaping. The drape is regularized and some care is given to the ultimate effect. The south Indian Brahmin, less active and more sedentary than the labourer, wears this more careful variant. Alternatively, with the use of a highly starched cotton or silk, or fine gilt brocade, another shape quite visually different is achieved.

The Thai pah-jungobein and the Cambodian sambot are tied basically in this same manner, with the difference that rather than crushing or twisting the ends, they are rigidly pleated and passed flatly through the legs.

As an extension of the hip wrap, a continuing length from the skirt can also be worn draped over the shoulder. This style is universal and as archaic in form as the extended wrap of early cultures. In its refined form it appears as the classical Roman toga and the Buddhist priest garb. The traditional female double wrap and its variations through to the modern sari are basically of this same mould.

In its simplest form a long length of cloth varying from three to six metres is first wrapped around the hips and secured at the waist; and the remainder of the cloth is then draped over one shoulder.

The modern sari is wrapped width-wise over an underslip and tucked into a drawstring waist-band, a safety-pin often being used at this point to secure the skirt portion. The plainer end of the fabric length is used for the lower wrap. The remaining length is measured over the shoulders and drawn to finger-tip length. Any excess fabric is gathered at mid-waist and folded over in pleats, falling free from the waist tuck. The reserved length is then drawn across the front of the body and draped over the left shoulder, dropping down the back to about seven-eighths the length of the skirt. The palu, or more elaborate end of the fabric, is used for this final shoulder fall.

The extended wrap or bronze toga of the Buddhist Thai priest uses much this same method. Styles of wrapping and arranging the cloth differ from sect to sect. It is at times fluid or strict, flat or folded. Often the final fall is wrapped around the waist. Women in particular wear the final length over the head. Field workers in the desert climate also use the final length as a protection against the sun. The loose end is often used as a handkerchief or as a general purpose rag. In south India an even longer length measuring up to nine metres is tied first as the dhoti or kanch tuck and then draped over the shoulder and finally banded around the waist.

As a variant of the extended wrap – as a separate length from the skirt – a shawl or cloak is draped over the shoulders. The chlamys and mantle of classic Greece, and the chadars and jamawars of northern India are all aspects of the shoulder wrap over a hip wrap or underskirt.

a

b

c

d

e

f

g

The Wrapped Garment

a

b

c

d

e

f

g

h

i

a *b* *c* *d* *e*

The draped unsewn costume developed primarily in mild or tropical climates. Its form is most typical of India and her sub-cultures in South-East Asia.

Of the two kinds of sewn garment, the closed sewn garment, simplified to its essentials, is composed of two woven lengths of equal proportions: one as the body shape, folded lengthwise at the shoulders, an opening cut for the neck, the other length cut in half across the width and folded as sleeves. These are set at right-angles in a T shape and sewn to the body portion. The sides and undersleeves are then sewn closed. The garment is slipped over the head. This is a development from the draped unsewn wraps; its seams are minimal and the end result is a loose-fitting garment. As an archetypal form it is basic to all of Asia, from the Kashmiri pheron to the Persian caftan and the ritual robes of imperial China.

Variations exist in the additional seamings and portions added to give more shape, ease or structural strength. Small triangles inserted as underarm gussets, or panels folded in bias wedges at the side seams are common additions.

When sewn garments are made up of worn-out draped lengths, as they often are, seams are used as a means of piecing together small remnants of cloth. Envelope folding, bias cuts, patched bits and pieces – whatever the base fabric is composed of – basically the form is folded and unseamed over the shoulder and the sleeves are extended from the body width. Hence visually the garment has an unfitted shoulder and a dropped sleeve inset seam. It gives a loose shape, often worn banded at the waist. The style is closed and it is slipped on over the head. Neck openings are varied. Ones large and circular, or slashed down the front or side, are particularly Indian in manner, and also apply to the T-shaped garments of Persia, Turkestan and the Caucasus. The closed Chinese robe, with a diagonal opening and an additional inner flap, is a further variant. This style is worn by both men and women. It is worn short as undergarment or shirt or long as a robe or in a caftan shape. A loose-fitting trouser wrapped and tied at the waist often complements the style.

The open sewn garment is most simply a divided or opened modification of the previous style. In its more complex form it is constructed of several widths of cloth, sewn lengthwise in multiple seams, and is essentially worn as an open coat, or cross-closed and sashed, over other garments.

The Persian loose open robe, the cross-closed waist-wrapped coat of the horse-proud cultures of north India and

a

b

c

d

China, or the Japanese kimono in its multiple forms – including the poetic excesses of the Fujiwara period where up to twenty garments were layered one over the other – are all variations on the same basic construction.

Originally the costume was brought to India with the Persian invasions in 516 BC where it took hold in the warrior class of northern India. It reappears as the later style of the angarkha of Rajasthan, as a refined modification of what was initially more rugged. As the long open coat layered over shorter undergarments including variants of breeches and trousers, its use extended as far as the influence of those Mongol horsemen – from the mountain tribes of middle Europe to the clans of the war lords of China.

A further extension is the sheathed costume. Fitted and tailored, or layered and wrapped closely to the body and limbs, it includes elements of all the previous styles. Though differing visually, the narrowed trouser and fitted achkan of the Indian upper class and the padded shields and armour of the samurai, with limbs in loose leggings, and calves bound in tight wrappings, are aspects of this form. Generally this more elaborate form was limited to the ruling or power classes. The introduction of tailoring and seamings fitted to the body was the result of Western influence. The Vietnamese aoidai and its Chinese prototype, the contemporary cheongsam, are in manner similar to the indigenous style, but the use of darts and shaped seams is a borrowed usage.

As a later mode, with the advent of European colonization and the arrival of the sewing machine, the use of body-hugging darts and shaped seams became more the manner of the cities and towns. Ordinary people in the villages and fields and on the mountain slopes of Asia have continued to wear the wrapped garments and the simple loose sewn garments.

a

b

c

d

e

f

g

h

i

32

a

b

c

d

e

f

g

The Courts

The King

The God King

The line of development that begins with the sorcerer and leads through the healing magician to the incarnate deity marks the growth of man's knowledge from the dark ages of fear. Man in the early stages of religious history saw himself as a feeble opponent of nature and devised protective magic to control and manipulate it. With the failure of magic as a consistent power, a more sophisticated ritual of prayer and sacrifice developed. Chosen men, the human deities, were believed to hold these controlling powers. This concept, that men may in fact achieve godliness through possession of divine powers, was a universally held belief.

As power often settles at the upper strata of society, it is usually within this area that the human divinity appears. The concept that kings possess supernatural powers, and specifically the ability to heal, was a universal one, and is still potent in portions of the world.

34

Asia has, within living memory, officially accepted the divine qualities of their kings as an integral part of the state religion. Belief in the divinity of kings was, however, held with more conviction and more broadly in the past, when the extension and survival of earlier theories of the living god in the person of the king was a vital part of Asian life. As with so many aspects of Asian life, the rural man in habits and beliefs still clings tenaciously to the older modes, whereas the urban Asian, like his European counterpart, in part pays respect to these traditions, and delights in the pageantry of kinghood, but with similar unconcern for the real meaning of the regal ceremony.

Symbols and notions of kingly behaviour and appearance have been entrenched in thousands of years of fairly static tradition. The deified rulers of the East were isolated from ordinary existence. Their lives were patterns of complicated protocol and highly ritualized behaviour. In some cases the ruler was in fact a political and religious leader; in others he was merely the symbol of power, with minimal direct leadership or power.

India has, perhaps, more than any other country in the world, been prolific in the creation of human gods. Divine grace has been liberally granted to all classes from kings to goatherds to resident foreign commissioners.

Strength, valour and the gifts of miraculous powers, albeit obscure and unsuspected, were the prerequisite qualities of human gods.

Early in Indian civilization the kings of the Gupta dynasty (AD 320–540) were often warriors. Strength and valour were by definition the qualities of the conqueror. If early rulers were not in fact the possessors of these traits, an attempt, particularly in their remaining sculpted and painted portrayals, was made to bestow these qualities on them.

The iconography of the gods was interchangeable with the manner of representing the kings. Though the ruler was sparsely clothed, he was richly decorated with the symbols of his office as the divine leader. In direct imitation of how the gods were visually imagined, the royal crown, his accoutrements and body jewels and ornaments echoed the detailed splendour of the deity. When the division between human and divine is blurred, the image of the divinity is draped and jewelled with more elaboration as the king himself devotes excessive attention to his appearance. In a sense, the god is viewed through man's limited concepts. The division in religious philosophies is a great deal more complicated than this simplified view suggests but it is true that the theory allowed the king to dress and behave in the image of what he felt his god to be.

With the invasion of the Muslims and their invisible god, the attempt to imitate godliness was limited to heroic manly qualities. More accurate portraits occur within the conventions of the Moghul court painters. The influence of Persia in medieval India was widespread. The Moghul ruler was robed in sewn garments, as opposed to the earlier drapes and wraps. Over fine muslin undergarments, the cross-closed robe was often in sheer, finely woven silk gauze, threaded with gold fibres and jewelled. The robe was sashed and girdled with costly scabbards and weapons. The accoutrements were now the symbols of the warrior and hunter. Sheer trousers were worn, in white muslin, either tight and gathered at the ankles or of more ample cut hanging fully below the robe.

Slippers of elongated cut were made of supple and decorated leathers. Headwraps and turbans replaced the earlier crowns and headdress. Turbans were often tied on frames before wearing. Egret and peacock feathers were mounted as standards. Pearls and gems were looped and studded in the turban folds. As in older styles, the body was hung with precious chains, the outer display was multiple necklaces, earstuds and rings. A major king, or Maharajah, was an impressive sight. Save for Elizabeth I or Louis XIV, the Sun King, there were no European monarchs to equal their costly splendour.

Despite the incredible wealth of jewels and fabric, the form and cut of the Moghul garment was fairly simple. As a variant of the Persian robe, the angarkha was cross-closed high up at the right shoulder and tied with long narrow tapes; or at times the neckline is deeper and curved. Further modifications occur when the waistline is delineated with a seam and the skirt portion is flared and gathered. Over-robes with fur additions are borrowed influences as well.

In some courts where the display of wealth was excessive, the kings were over-indulged. Due to a rich diet of pleasures, the rigours of manly battle and the hunt were more the eulogies of official poets than realities. Obesity and indolence amongst royalty were common and therefore idealized. Even the architecture reflects the intricate patterns of pleasure, the plots and subterfuges. More lively rulers and their courts,

a

b

c

d

e

f

g

36

h

i

j

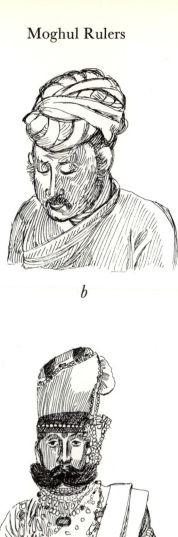

a

b

c

d

e

f

g

h

however, held the simpler sports of hunting and hawking, riding and war as activities worthy of kingly excellence. Their active life is reflected in the shorter robe, trousers and boots. The costume is an extremely refined development of that of the earlier horsemen. Contrasted with the more sedentary ruler, comfortably nested in pillows and wide-based low thrones, the young prince or sportsman king was less jewelled and turbans are smaller and tighter wrapped. Ears were often wholly or partially exposed; boots replaced the slippered foot. At this time the clean-shaven fashion sported in preceding reigns gave way to elaborate beard and moustache styles.

The opulence of the king was reflected in the styles of his court; however, the king was set apart. The 'halo of divinity' used by Moghul portrait artists designates him as a god king.

The Son of Heaven

Despite the vastness of her land area and her immense population China developed a uniformity of ethics and culture, shaped by an intense sense of tradition as an unbroken chain linking the remote past to the present.

Styles of dress would vary, not so much from area to area, nor from outside influences, but most strongly according to social rank. Rising from the massive base of land labourers and the village population, the imperial court dominated the immense pyramid of stratified ranks. The emperor himself was more than a human ruler; he was a symbol, and titled the 'Son of Heaven'; he was believed to inherit his supreme position directly from the 'Sovereign on High'.

The early Shang buried their dead kings as gods and the royal burials were accompanied by large-scale human sacrifice. Offerings of riches were interred with the king. Bronze vessels, pottery, carved implements and jewellery of jade and marble, fabric, musical instruments and weapons of war were buried with the king to secure his passage to heaven

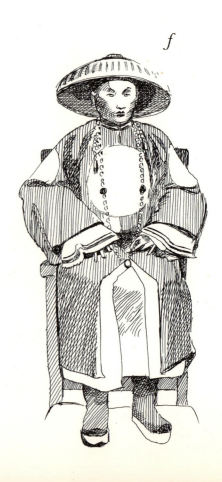

a

b   d

c

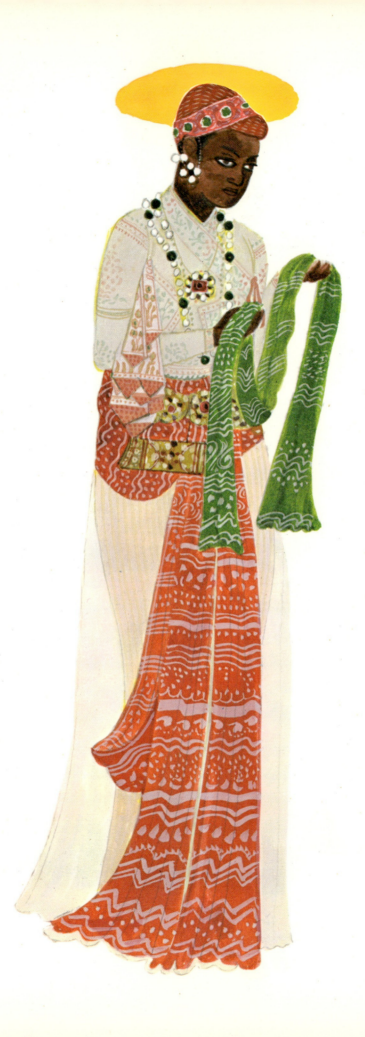

and assure his position among the gods. Early philosophy was an elaboration on the implications of the death of a monarch: ancestor worship and the divinity of kings developed to more sophisticated levels over the centuries. By the time of the Ch'in (221 BC) the emperor had come to be seen as the power linking heaven and earth. Symbols of his kingship and the dense philosophy that supported the ideal of the celestial ruler also prevailed over his human qualities. The emperor would often fulfil the role demanded of him as poet and sage, qualities which were regarded as appropriate to a divine ruler.

The fluid robes of the early dynasties disappear with the strict and rigid shape of the imperial Dragon Robe and its austere conventions. Elaborate patterns appear on the imperial robe, not as random decorations, but as juxtaposed motifs reflecting the theology of earth, sky, sun and moon. The divine balance of these aspects was conventionalized and each symbol had ritual meaning. Waves, bordered at the hem of the gown and at sleeve bands, are a stylized representation of the sea. From this base motif, a mountain rises as the earth sign, and above are clouds signifying heaven. Dragons, usually nine in number, represent the emperor as the Son of Heaven. Dragons predominate on the body of the robe, and entwined among the clouds and dragons are other auspicious symbols such as bats, cranes, flowers and swastikas.

The imperial garment was in shape and cut not unlike the robe of the courtier or provincial gentry. What set it apart was the quality of fabric, the iconography of the patterned motifs and colouring, symbolic of rank. Only the immediate delegates of the imperial authority, the mandarin and the high officials, would wear robes of similar complexity. The elongated sleeves, often completely concealing the hands, were either simply extended lengths or prolonged undergarments. The 'hoof' sleeve cuff was a curved cut addition and was extended over the hands like horses' hooves. Hats and headdresses were styled strictly to rank, jewels and feathers distinctly marking the level of authority. Jewellery was held to be precious but was comparatively simple. Empresses wore similar gowns, corresponding in shape and details to the male robe. The addition of over-robes and tippets was common. Fur trims and linings were used for the winter months.

The emperor and his consort in nineteenth-century portraits are visualized as austere but baroque symbols of earthly and celestial power. The shape of the body is entirely obscured by clothing. Even the face is smoothed and stretched with a heavy layer of rice powder. The individual is almost obliterated in the stylized façade of a divine image. Glimpses of long fingernails and ringed fingers are the only hint of the frail human within the massive gown. Feet are concealed in rounded hoof-like slippers mounted on padded platforms. The overall image implies rigid power equally dominant in worldly and heavenly spheres.

The Earthly Counterpart

Japanese society was strongly influenced by Chinese thought and culture, by the philosophy of Confucius, ancestor worship and obedience to the emperor. With the influx of Buddhism from India during the Nara period (in the years 676–710) the emperor was seen as the earthly counterpart of the Buddha.

Japan's warrior cult figured so prominently that the soldier was to be of prime importance in the power structure. Unlike the position in China, the warrior class – the samurai and the shogun at its head – was to achieve actual governing power.

The costume conventions of the Japanese imperial court bring an abstract sense to the almost total obliteration of the human form and proportion.

In the Tokugawa period (1615–1867) the emperor appeared as a purely symbolic entity. Lip service was paid to his divine descent but the power of government was in the hands of the shogun and the military. Though he remained titular head of state, the emperor was scarcely portrayed as pictures of him were taboo.

The baroque, heavily patterned complexities of China are simplified and broadened in Japan. Ritual, and to a lesser extent aesthetics, dictated that the colours used be predominantly plain, as each colour was officially prescribed as an index of rank. For example, the dominant colours of royalty were red, purple and blue; and white, as the ceremonial colour, was forbidden to the merchant class.

The ceremonial robe of the Japanese court was developed from the Chinese robe. Cross-closed to a high rolled and padded collar it was open as a coat, but in effect was closed: double folded in a panel at the front. (The diagonal closure of the Chinese robe is echoed in the court kimono of the warrior class.) Sleeves are voluminous and stiffly pleated at the sleeve join. The effect is severe and unadorned with surface decorations or patterns. Jewellery is non-existent. Headgear is patterned after the early Chinese modes of the Sung. Styles are sleek, black lacquered shapes. A starched gauze panel in sheer black rises over the stiffened form, creating a starkly theatrical effect. The volume of the costume is out of proportion to the human frame, and in the Heian period is excessive to the point of overwhelming the body with multiple layers.

An image of perfection is created by an Asian monarch's costume. With the unlimited uses of wealth and culture, the craft of clothing and decoration is extended to ever-new refinement. The kingly garment can be seen as an extension of the separate philosophies and ideals. At the base of the pyramid of power the masses, restricted by the limitations of a life of very different pressures, assume other qualities and the intrinsic ideal of dress is only minimally reflected. But among the middle strata of society the urge to mirror these ultimate values is stronger, and so on upwards to the narrower confines of power.

48

The Courtiers

The Indian Court

If the ruler seated on the regal throne depicted the ideal of the culture, the court that surrounded him represented in many cases the actual power. Although the elaborate courtly system of India reflected the wealth and manners of the monarch, traditionally the aristocracy claimed moral, spiritual and literary leadership for itself. Though there were those who set themselves ideals of dignified authority, these ideals were not always followed in practice.

The ancient Indians, as well as the Moghul courts, placed great value on flowers and trees. Their leisure gardens were planned expanses of fragrant trees and flowers. Artificial lakes and pools, sequestered pavilions, fountains and bathing tanks, pleasure swings, the attributes of music and poetry, set the scene for the courtly joys both profane and profound.

In contrast to these agreeable pastimes, the realities of power often led to armed conflicts. Medieval Indian armies were fighting forces of immense numbers. Cavalry elephant platoons and foot soldiers together would number up to a million strong.

As an extension of the court culture, the power systems of more recent and contemporary times must deal with problems accumulated over the centuries, even though the rigid caste systems of traditional status and wealth are all but extinguished. Power in India today, as in any other modern culture, is often in the hands of the wealthy, but the intellectual, the politician and the leaders of society cross barriers that centuries ago would have been insurmountable.

The influence of the Hindu courts was very strong in the royal courts of the Indian sub-cultures in South-East Asia. It was to separate the aristocracy even more from the general populace, who followed other religious and cultural patterns. But today the patterns of power there owe more to Western politics than to their Indian heritage.

a

b

c

d

e

a

b

c

d

e

f

g

h

a

b

c

d

e

f

g

h

54

a

b

c

d

e

f

g

h

a

b

c

d

e

a

b

c

d

e

f

g

The Celestial Courts of China

The harsher climate, both real and metaphoric, produced a courtly culture in China very different from the idyllic softer tones of the Indian Court. The roots of Chinese culture grew deep in times of peace, more twisted and devious in times of stress and conflict.

Mongol and Turkish conquerors, harsh and aggressive, brought constant revitalization to courts settled to an over-refined luxury hard-won from a hostile environment. In contrast, the Indian sub-continent absorbed invaders in its all-embracing culture: though the invaders' influence was more strongly but superficially marked in the courts, their traces were all but obliterated in the slow and unremitting pace of Indian history. The Chinese court and culture, on the other hand, were pulled up by the roots and the 'barbarian' influence in their replacement was strong and deep.

The Buddhist monk Fa-hsien, who came from China and recorded the life of fifth-century India, was to compare the orderly and benevolent civilization of the Gupta Empire with the time of troubles, between the great periods of the Han and the T'ang, in China.

Chinese society's strict hierarchy was elaborately displayed in the courtly costume. Rank and position were marked by symbolic patterns, colours and garments. It would have been unthinkable to exceed one's rank in the detail of costume, though in actual fact with aristocratic intrigues that were an integral part of court life rank was surpassed in other ways.

The niceties of courtyard and gardens, the grace and refinement of a civilization that abounded in the accumulated wealth of trade and conquest – these were always in danger from the cruelty and comparative vulgarity of the invaders from the north.

Present-day power is in direct and pointed opposition to all that preceded. However, the attempt to erase the distinctions of status in modern China by eradicating dress differences has in effect not been unlike the traditional and ancient methods. Fundamentally the Chinese costume was always in its basic form and shape the same. It was the details of fabric and the additional touches of luxury that provided the differences. The Chinese industrialist, even in the new context of the communist state, is still, in his 'Mao' jacket and trousers, a great distance from his brother in the fields with essentially the same outfit.

a

b

c

d

e

f

g

h

i

j

k

l

m

a

b

c

d

e

f

g

h

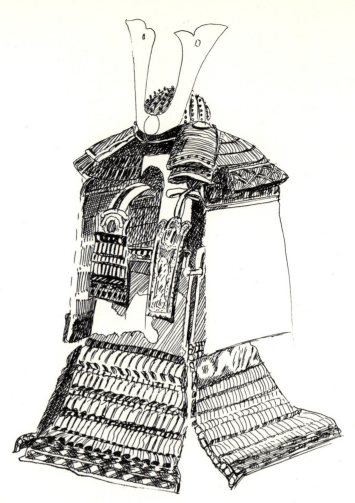

The Warrior Court of Japan

The thread that runs throughout the fabric of Japanese culture – idealization of the imperfect – is at its highest level in courtly and ceremonial attitudes. With an instinct for detail that is unparalleled in other cultures, the Japanese have lifted beauty out of mundane and ordinary objects and have achieved balance and harmony in asymmetry. The enigma of contradiction forms the base of Japanese philosophy.

Worship of purity and refinement, the inheritance from China, was to survive and outlive its origins. By long isolation Japan gained the required privacy to extend and detail her heritage.

Disparities of illusion and truth were nowhere more strongly marked than in the court. With an almost theatrical display of good taste and *politesse*, and formality and precision of manners, the nuances and shades of meaning are deep and hidden under the surface lacquer.

As early as the Nara period in the sixth century, control was in the hands of the shogun, the war lords, or in the power of the civil regents who ruled behind the name of the emperor. This feudal system of actual power behind the throne was to continue with vigorous regularity throughout the succession of civil wars and uprisings into modern times.

Screening the brutal undulations of power, a formalized court pondered the placid choices that the highly ritualized life offered. The finest skills were expended in adapting and refining. Shape was placed against shape, colour juxtaposed gracefully to its highest harmonious balance and syllables and phrases were worked with equal pleasure. Craftsmen excelled in the manipulation of brush work and the arduous skills of woodblocking. All gave the effect of spontaneous ease, all to the exquisite end of small and precise joys. The adventurous and bold were the exception. Yet out of this attention to detail has come certainly a costume culture surpassing all others in pure and stable beauty.

a

b

c

d

e

f

g

a

b

c

d

e

f

a

b

c

d

e

f

68

a

b

c

d

e

f

g

h

a

b

c

d

e

f

g

The Inner Chamber

Polygamy was often the rule for the Asian courts, though this practice did not necessarily extend to the general people. The popular religions often proscribed it, or economics limited the habit. The practice of concubinage in China, the multiple wives of the Siamese and the Indonesian rulers and the inner chamber or women's quarters in Moghul India led to dress habits that supported the system.

In India, particularly in the north where the Muslims took firm hold, the Moghul conquest brought cumbersome, concealing garments to replace the more revealing dress of the Hindu and Buddhist societies. Jewellery, under the Moghuls, was often a form of decorated shackle; in extreme cases it hindered movement considerably. Similarly, the practice of binding feet in China, aside from an erotic intent, was intended to restrict the movements of a woman. Exaggeratedly lengthened robes in Japan were so restricting that they only allowed simpering gestures. Clothing reflected an ambiguous ideal: woman was at once a goddess and a slave, a saint and a strumpet.

Despite the fact that they were generally held to be men's subordinates, the rights and privileges enjoyed by women varied from age to age. In pre-Muslim India women of the courts or the wealthy bourgeoisie were often well versed in the arts and literature. Despite the taboo against educating ladies in later Moghul times and up to very recent past, the arts of music, singing and the dance were considered lady-like pursuits. It is true that at some times women were partners in sport and war and that the early Mauran kings were guarded by a troupe of Amazons, but these provide the exception, not the rule.

Although under the harsher terms of seclusion in other areas of the Orient, women found within their limited horizons a species of security and exercised a surreptitious sort of power. As in early India, the courtesans of China and Japan were highly literate and in some cases the social system disguised a matriarchal society where women held the real power.

Nowadays the more rigid aspects of polygamy and the limited role in society accorded women are by and large habits of the past. The modern world looks askance at what was certainly in its more extreme forms a species of slavery. But the practice of Muslim purdah is still practised in parts of Asia, and even today one can see remnants of the older customs. Tough street workers and burly country women coquettishly hide their faces behind their extended wraps.

A mincing manner and falsetto whine, lending a kind of 'southern' charm, can be found amongst many Thai women. Rural Japanese and Chinese women have modest manners in counterpoint to their more liberated city sisters. Raucous market women, henpeckers, and shrill money-handlers one can assume always existed.

a

b

c

d

e

f

g

h

i

j

k

74

a

b

c

d

e

f

g

h

a

b

c

d

e

f

76   g

h

a

b

c

d

e

f

a

b

c

d

e

f

78

The Temple

As in the church and the temple the world over, the past survives intact in the rituals of religious practices.

Asian temples have been protected by their insular nature from the upheavals of social change. Vestiges of clothing habits of ancient times have remained to the present day. The varying ideals are still supported, and, unlike their counterparts in the West, religion, philosophy and magic are in the atmosphere and live deep in the fibre of everyday Asian life.

As one imagines it might have been in biblical times, in India the streets are full of prophets and ascetics. The villages as well as the cities support the mendicants, the soothsayers and the sages, and dress five millenniums old moves unnoticed among the Terylene business suits.

In contrast to a European cathedral, a Buddhist temple is essentially unstructured and casual, reflecting the more open-ended quality of Buddhist practices. Particularly in Thailand and Burma, the temple is a sedate meeting place, where gossip, magic and mystery gather all at once. In these countries all young men are called to Buddhist monkhood for a period of a few months rather in the manner of national service, with the result that ordinary people become intimate with its garb and principles. A more ritualistic Buddhism in the Himalayas, coupled with older pagan practices, thrives in a climate of everyday magic, and the overlay of the neighbouring mountain cultures of China – a mixture of ancient cults and secular practices – produces a religious costume that is a startling contrast to the more benign traditions of the southern Buddhist. In the context costume tradition is more complex.

The shamans of earlier times, the priest of more sophisticated cults, the odd Westerner from Idaho looking for the middle way, all reflect the adherence to the past and to a future free of the complexities of modern times.

a

b

c

d

e

f

g

h

a

b

c

d

e

f

g

a

b

c

d

e

f

g

h

The Theatre

Indian Theatre

Indian theatre as a developed convention was an aristocratic pastime. From its early roots as a popular form of entertainment of ritual mime, song and dance, it grew through a form of religious offering and edification until it reached its classic form as a highly developed minority culture in the palaces and the temples.

Before it attained this level of sophistication, theatre was not unlike its present-day form in rural India and South-East Asia. Travelling groups of entertainers endured a rough-and-tumble life, living from festivals and wedding parties.

Dating from the first century AD the religious dramas, the romantic tales of gods and goddesses, adventure epics of godly princes and demons and the classic tale of the

Ramayana were literary products of the monarch and his court. Temple and courtly drama was almost exclusively dedicated to religious themes. Secular topics were mostly dramas of historical kings and light comedies of harem intrigue; even these were moralities, and the recurrent theme of the victory of good over evil was often presented in a flamboyant, romantic, comic or horrific manner. Convention did not allow tragedy, and although tragic scenes and high melodrama were common enough, endings were invariably happy (a tradition that seems to have survived in present-day popular Indian films).

Normally dramas were performed privately in the courts and in the houses of the wealthy, or were given public showings in temple courtyards on festival days. There was no regular theatre, only wandering troupes of professionals, in the manner of the European medieval strolling players. A play would be performed without scenery and with a minimum of stage properties.

Costuming was strictly conventional, so that heroes, heroines, gods and demons were immediately recognizable. Mythological and religious themes were costumed after the attire of the heroic kings of early India, but these costumes become so stylized that one cannot regard them as historically accurate. Styles differed as theatrical and dance groups developed throughout the kingdoms. Local and contemporary dress was always an influential element.

As in Indian dance, there is a complicated code of hand, facial and body gestures, capable of conveying not only a wide range of emotions, but the more abstract qualities of mood and temper; gestures could also symbolize plants and animals. A well-trained audience could recognize from the gestures of the actor that the king was riding a chariot through a forest, or that the dancers' movements described a faun in fright or a god seeking his revenge. The ancient rules of the Bharata Natyasastra codify thirteen postures of the head, thirty-six of the eyes, nine of the neck, thirty-seven of the hand and ten of the body. Later dance texts classify many more, each pose and gesture signifying a specific emotion or object.

The oldest form of traditional Indian dancing was a personification of the god Krishna by temple priestesses, the Devadasi. As an outgrowth of this the classical Bharata Nhatyam was performed as an Hindu act of religious piety. Another important style is the Muslim Kathak, which was a Moghul courtly entertainment. Gradually over the centuries as dancers left the temples and courts and began to travel the country on a freelance basis, dance became a much despised art, for in the public's mind it was inseparable from prostitution. Only very recently has the theatre become an acceptable art for women, during the resurgence of the classical dance and singing in the last fifty years. Another recent innovation is the interest in folk theatre and dancing as an organized theatrical event.

The theatrical culture of Ceylon, Thailand and Indo-China is almost purely an Indian heritage. The folk theatres of Thailand and Indo-China, however, owe more in their form to the Chinese. A village 'like' in Thailand or an outdoor festival performance in India is a long many-hour affair. For a western observer there are the distractions of incidental din and commotion, of an audience far more varied than the usual 'theatre-going crowd': infants at breast and unattended children in full mischief amongst supine loungers in deep sleep, and hordes of food and snacks. Unlike theatre in the West and in the more ritualized theatre in Japan, the Asian audience is not a captive one. Full attention is expected and received only when the performers demand it. As an extension of the private performance, theatre for the untutored is often considered as 'background music' and as such is enjoyed with relish and without the solemn rites of the aesthete. However, a very numerous exception is the connoisseur, well-trained to appreciate every nuance. As an intense auditeur he is ready to recognize skill, and with clicks and head nods encourages the accomplished artist.

a

b

c

d

e

f

87

a

b

c

d

e

f

g

a

b

c

d

e

f

a

b

c

d

e

f

a

b

c

d

e

f

g

a

b

c

d

e

f

g

93

a

b

c

d

e

Chinese Theatre

The musicians of the Shang kings were courtly favourites, and as early as 700 BC mixed theatricals, combining pantomime, singing, dancing and acrobatics were popular entertainments. Feats of a purely physical nature have always been a strong element in Chinese folk theatre. The Chinese circus, as well, is a folk culture descended from ancient times.

The formal theatre dates from the time of Emperor Ming Huang when a dramatic academy was set up in the Pear Garden of the Imperial Park. From it issued the classical form of the eighth-century T'ang which was to form the foundation of Chinese traditional theatre.

As in India, Chinese theatre had always been performed in three separate environments: in the courts, temples and in the open air as public festivities. The religious aspect is less persistent and themes are divided into categories of Military or Civil, which were respectively tragic or comic.

Military themes were on grandiose and tragic scale, involving the conquest of kings and elaborate subplots of court intrigue. Comedies and farces were often petty involvements of tax collectors, minor provincial governors, and heroic fishermen.

Similar in this respect to Western ballet, the conventions of the Chinese theatre are not realistic. The audience does not expect a literal but rather a poetical translation of reality. Conventions of time and logic are more abstract than actual. Both in costume and make-up there is a purely formal symbolism of colour:

red – loyalty, sacredness or divine qualities
purple – as red but to a lesser degree
black – indicates good but rather uncouth characters
blue – tiger-like ferocity, craftiness, haughtiness and so on
yellow – all the qualities of blue but to a lesser degree
green – an unstable and unreliable character
orange and pale grey – old age or infirmity.

Japanese Theatre

Japanese drama prior to the Meiji restoration in the nineteenth century consisted of three main types of performance: the Noh play, the Kabuki, and the puppet drama or Jōruri. Noh, the earliest of the three, was a product of a long and gradual development. The first shaping factors on its growth were the eleventh-century farces known as Kyogen, which were to survive more serious derivatives and are still performed as interludes between Noh plays. They were to some extent displaced by religious plays depicting Buddhist legends for the populace, which soon spread beyond the confines of religious themes. When in the fifteenth century themes of beauty, silence and solitude took precedence over religious teaching the drama became Noh. The entire repertoire of present-day Noh can be credited to four members of a single family of actors, an enlightened despot who was their patron, and a span of eighty years during which time they wrote all the plays that form the unchanging Noh canon.

Noh is the oldest living drama in the world today, having survived virtually intact as a theatrical museum for four hundred years. The all-male drama makes use of masks and theatrical symbolism. Costume traditions are strictly adhered to, each character and type being limited by rigid conventions. Noh's audience was the nobility and the warrior class, for whom it was the only type of theatre that they were officially allowed to patronize. Today it is a theatre of such minority taste that for the simple observer it is no more than a display of brilliant but controlled colour and costume, performed at a slow pace and opaque with symbols both visual and aural. In the seventeenth century, with the development of Kabuki and Jōruri, most of the audience deserted Noh and it became exclusively aristocratic, which is how it remains today – a theatre for the intelligentsia.

Kabuki has become the Japanese popular theatre as its form is more vigorous and less astringent. The costume tradition was an outgrowth of the Noh, but as a more flexible tradition existed more innovations were made. The art of dance is essential to Kabuki and the rich visual effects seem to override its basic themes of loyalty and piety, cruelty and violence.

Japanese theatre reaches its height in Jōruri. An illusion of life is accomplished through exaggerated conventions despite seemingly impossible obstacles. The puppet manipulators are fully visible, and scene and costume changes are made in full view of the audience. The puppets are almost life-size, and the themes are larger-than-life tragedies. But all the elements together create a strange paradox – the puppets seem to be bursting with colour and life, and their manipulators seem to disappear, invisible in their symbolic black cloth.

a

b

c

d

e

f

g

a

b

c

d

e

f

g

The Villages

India: Landscape and People

From the wooded slopes to the mountain peaks of Kashmir, a clear open sky arches over a black and white landscape. The predominantly neutral tones are sharply shadowed. People wear white and black. Colour, when it is used, is hesitant and half-way. Sharp- and gaunt-featured pale people look like biblical characters.

The Rajasthan desert is burnt and arid. The Rajput villages are masonry-walled towns rising from the dusty earth. The people, as an affront to the sun-bleached sky, dress in a burst of bright colour: intense tones of greasy pink and sharp greens; reds like oxen; blood-yellows from timid to raucous varieties; whites that are dingy but contrast sharply with the brown skins. Faces are full, handsome and heavily featured. Women are particularly noticeable, flaunting and arrogant. Their heavy skirts swing from ample hips. Their strong backs are arched in the balanced gait of the pot carrier. Men wear jaunty turbans piled and twisted in disorderly fashion, in whites, pinks and oranges as a bright topping on their stick-like forms. Field workers are bird-like in the traditional, baggy and haphazard dhoti. The Muslim women are like dark shadows in black. As throughout the length of India, fabric is everywhere, stretched out to dry in colourful streaks on river banks.

Following the Ganges further east, the intensity of the holy city Benares is magnified by the hollow faces of the crowds, the colours of decay, all shades and conditions of white. The ascetic, gnarled and marked, is hung with tatters like the temple trees. This is a secluded world of religious ardour, retired from worldly activities; figures in this landscape are silent effigies in classical and oppressive drapery.

To Lucknow and a more affluent atmosphere of gentle ruin. Ageing prosperous residences are overgrown by voluptuous gardens, remnants of Victorian splendour. The busy commercial quarters are in garish colours, and the little lean-to shops are burdened with the confusion of modern with the old. Shopkeepers, typical throughout India, are perched on slightly raised platforms. They sit cross legged on prosperous hips amongst the cacophony of their wares, patient and wily. The French, Italians and the English have left their reminders. The self-effacing and over-polite Lucknow gentility retire to the niceties of deep-shadowed rooms, encumbered with victoriana. A has-been Begum with heavy kholled eyes, and powder greying a faded and aristocratic face, receives for tea in an exquisitely embroidered sari which is yellowed and stained. Dapper men wear sheer white shirts in the early morning, crisp and starched over the tight-legged churida, which quickly soften and age to crumpled and genteel limpness by sundown.

To Madras in the south-east where the fields open up to long lengths of bright young green. Tall palms rise above the rice paddies and bleached white Georgian relics. Here colour comes as an echo from the northern deserts. The village people are spare and small boned, brilliant and dark. More perverse combinations of colour vie with whites. Poison greens, deep aubergine, deep blues from clear open to purpled midnights set against oranges and chrome yellows. Bottle green and crimson red. Vivid browns against dense pinks. Cerise, mauve and purple. Peacock, royal purple, orange and acid pink. Inner streets are like ancient Pompeii, sculptural buff-walled houses, opening up to views of family life in recessed courtyards.

And across to Kerala on the opposite coast, red-earthed and full green. The rolling hills are cut, gouged and squared to neat bordered plots. A variety of trees and leaves; polished and feathery, the palms and underbrush, a tangle of luxurious greenery. White and trim houses of simple prosperity, churches and spires in whitewash sit in the jungle like tame house cats. People are burnished and deepest brown. Here whites are blazing chalk whites or milky and creamy. Middle-class burghers are rather dumpy in Christian whites with black umbrellas, women in cumbersome saris. The village women are in tame colours, not in the vivid contrasts of Madras. The pot bearers are much less extravagant of gesture, but modest and mincing like the little village goats, small-boned and delicate. Children are everywhere, in their serious school uniforms, the girls in bright hair bows. Laden with books, they have a bright-eyed liveliness that betrays their orderly appearance on country roads. On this southern coast, the men are the most striking. Long and lean or square and solid, they have the good looks, spare and clearly drawn features that set apart the fleshy nose, puffy cheeks and baroque faces of the north as visibly foreign. Men are gaceful dandies in the simplest clothes; the white shirt and long lunghi skirt. The constant folding and tying, lifting and tucking brings a grace to the ordinary and commonplace. As in all of India, one sees in the villages the repetitious rhythm of simple life intact over the centuries.

a

b

c

d

e

f

g

h

a

b

c

d

e

f

g

a

b

c

d

e

f

g

South India

III

Indian Decorations

a

b

c

d

e

f

g

h

i

j

a

b

c

d

e

f

g

h

i

j

When clothing has to be purely functional, when it has to either protect the body from a harsh climate or shield it from the sun, the number of forms and designs it can take is restricted. The working dress of the field is limited by the purposes it serves and is simplified to essentials. The elementary body wraps are common to many areas as the simple solution to a widespread problem.

When there is an urge to decorate or expand beyond the straightforward forms of utility, then there is scope for a wealth of diversity and a richness of detail. This extension from the purest and simplest produces decorative aspects that are particular to regions or express the more extensive needs of more complex cultures. Magic and religion, hierarchy and status, and the impulse of allurement are further demands beyond those of pure utility. Man does not prepare a list of his essentials and his luxuries and proceed to design to order; instead the list grows as his culture develops and answers are found to its needs.

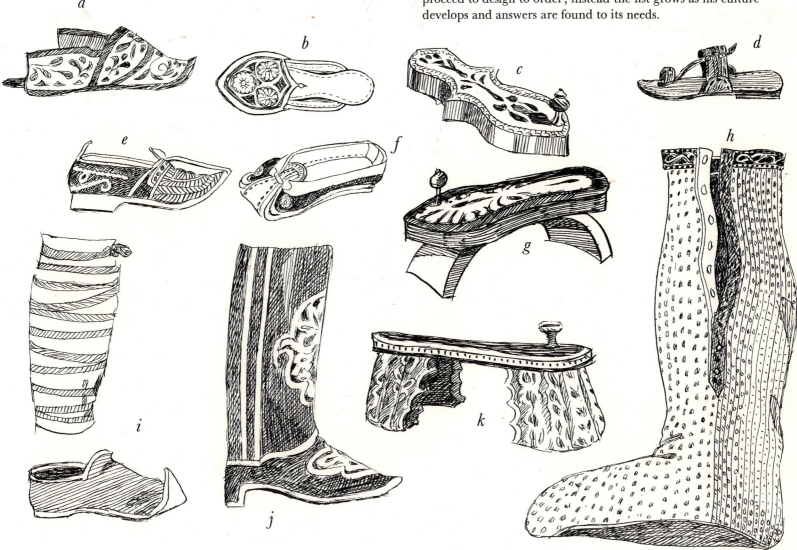

a

b

c

d

e

f

g

h

i

j

k

a

b

c

d

e

Details

a

b

c

e

d

f

a

b

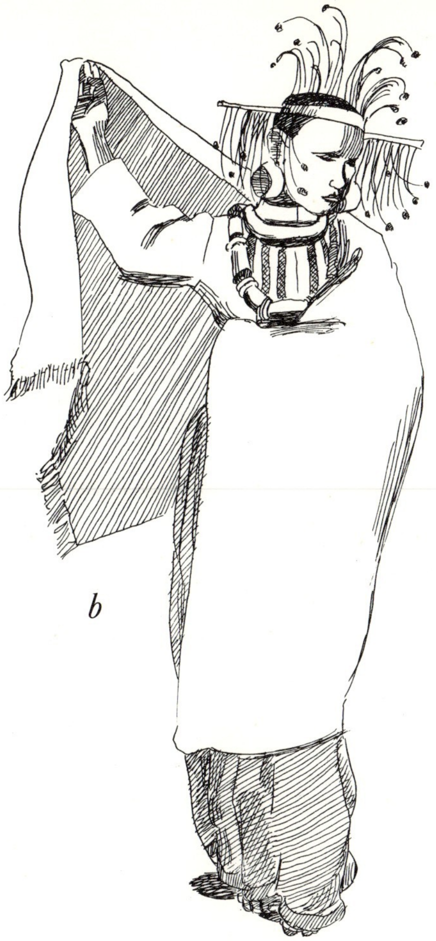

c

d

e

f

g

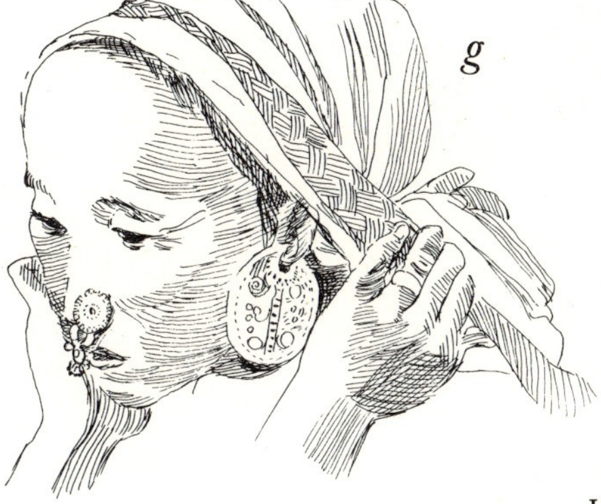

a

b

c

d

e

f

g

a

b

c

d

e

f

g

h

a

b

c

d

e

f

g

h

Out of the Past

The secluded villages all across Asia are like tarnished mirrors of the past. In the hill and mountain ranges, suffering the cold winds and given to the mysteries of the awe-inspiring space and solitude of the distant peaks, in the fertile valleys and plains, villages recessed in the fields bypassed by the commercial highways, in the desert stretches, where villages huddle in clusters, crumbling walled fortresses against the ancient marauders who have found safer livelihoods in the cities, when change comes it is like a river, bringing the enrichment of progress to some and inundation and ruin to others.

Tribal communities living in remote hills and forests have survived the centuries but their tribal folklore and culture are threatened by the inevitable present. They exist as prehistoric remnants in a changing world. The Adivasis of India, the hill tribes of Thailand and Burma, the mountain tribes of China and Japan are precarious cultures and vulnerable populations in areas of transition.

The settled farmers and village dwellers have, by and large, the religious and life values of medieval cultures that have resisted, but slowly absorbed, the modes of the changing world. The wooden plough gives way to the tractor, the traditional clothes of antiquity to the costume of the town, with less trauma than the ritual habits of the Iron Age to the modern mysteries of the transistor radio and folding money.

In the isolated villages the innate good sense of ancient clothing has resisted the advance of snap fasteners and metal zips. Costume traditions embedded in custom have survived the universal uniform. The old crafts of weaving, printing and embroidering are still remembered and followed, but in areas of change these skills give way with astonishing speed to manufactured goods and sleazy imitations.

Jewellery as a visible show of possessions, and the enjoyment of casual and precious decoration and the habits of barter are only slowly being replaced by monetary and banking systems. In the wealth of everyday details as a reminder of the past, the deep sense of tradition is tenacious and intact.

But as tribal peoples occupy territory rich in forest and water resources, minerals and metals, their days of ignorance and innocence are numbered. As villages are drawn into activities of national life, as communications with town and city spread, the slow tempo of change is quickened.

An Overall View

Though rural costumes have local characteristics supported by centuries of habit, one can see overriding the variations similarities rising from parallels of climate and social situation. The interchange of historical trade and conquest overlaps present boundaries.

In the northernmost borderlands of India, and more remotely within the hill villages of Nepal, Bhutan, Sikkim, Tibet and Manchuria, history has produced a mixture of cultures in which the religions of the Buddhist, the Hindu, the Muslim and the shaman cults of animist beliefs all thrive. Clothes reveal an equal variety of origins. The basic cross-closed garment found in these regions is essentially Mongol Chinese. The layered shawls and drapery, the tippets, wrapped aprons and cummerbunds, the heavy boots and distinctive headwear are remnants of the Tibetan and Chinese caravan trade. Padded and layered clothing is typical and natural to cold climates. Wearing hot iron warmers in folds of clothing is common in Kashmir as it is in Tibet. The habit of very infrequent bathing is also common to these mountain climates. Fabrics are often lacquered with grease, and colours are faded or enriched with age. Clothing worn by horsemen and shepherds is rough textured and hardy, silks and gauzed fabrics are the additional choices for the landowners and the sedentary. Heavy boots are both the result of the nomadic cultures and their dependence on the horse and the requirements of harsh climate. The distinctive headgear, as useful clothing, is protective against the cold. Particularly for the ears, flaps and wraps are common. (In the West, at the first sign of cold, hands are protected with gloves and mittens. Ears in Asia seem a first priority, and even in the cities when sweaters are worn under rayon suiting, a woollen scarf is tied kerchiefwise over turbans and Muslim caps.) Hats and headdress in its more decorative forms classify rank and class in the Chinese manner with distinctive tassles and buttons.

Among the nomadic mountain people brocaded silks and finely woven fabrics are used for ceremonial robes, but as weaving in the farther stretches of the mountain cultures is unknown they are often the remnants of old mandarin robes.

However, simple looms, often portable or of the back-strap variety, produce heavy wool or goat fibre fabrics. Remnant silk or cotton is pieced and patched as brilliant touches. Jewellery is heavy and of large and bold design. It is hardly ever purely decorative, but worn as protective amulets or as indications of rank.

In essence the hill villages all along the mountain ranges of Asia are typified by layered, cross-closed garments with additional waist ties and shoulder wraps. Padded felt or leather boots are worn under the long robes. Clothing styles are similar for men and women. Headgear both wrapped and sewn, hair arrangements and ornate hair ornaments are typically distinctive of area and caste.

Deeper in the warmer valleys and fields, working clothing is geared to active agricultural tasks rather than the watching and waiting of animal-tending. The climate is kinder, and aside from the hazards of nature, life is easier. The skirt and trouser wraps – the dhoti, the lunghi and sarong of India and her sub-cultures, the shawls and extended wraps – and the sewn garments – shirts and jackets, the drawstring trousers and long full skirts – are the products of centuries of a comparative stability in the villages for all the changes at court and throne. Equally ageless are the working clothes of China, in the almost solitary style of the 'coolie' jacket and trousers for both men and women, and the varied clothing of Japanese farmers and fishermen in combinations of cloth and straw, animal and fish skins, and beaten bark fibre – exceptions to this temperate climate's staple fabric of cotton.

Head wraps range from the simple head tie across the brow in south India, South-East Asia and across to China and Japan, to the elaborate turban styles of India. Head wraps are often simple protection against heat and rain, but turban styles in their more complicated forms are indications of sect and class. In the terraced or flat rice fields of Asia protection against the elements is afforded by the wide-sloped straw hats. Feet are bare or sandled. Leather and fibre styles exist when weather demands protection from rain or mud.

In areas of intense heat, in arid climates, clothing is usually layered and covered against the sun, full and loose on the body. The heavy skirts and head shawls of Rajasthan and the shrouded Muslim robes are typical of this approach. Bare torsos and minimal clothing are more common to the areas of moist heat and monsoon. Abbreviated hip wraps and simple loin cloths are used by both sexes. The male and female skirt is tied tightly across the hips but the long loose ends lift with the odd breeze. Fabric after repeated washings is fluid and cooling. Shirts and bodices are often loose and of thin gauze-like fabric. Tight body-hugging shirts and cropped bodices are often in bias cuts allowing wide movements, or are patched when movements go beyond the allowance of the cut.

Particularly in south India and South-East Asia, clothing is washed often out of pride and habit. Cleanliness is comfort in the humid areas of Asia. Flowers and sweet-smelling accessories are used by both men and women. Jewellery is more decorative, though ritual as well, and often very finely wrought.

Traditional village costumes have survived because they are successful adaptations to specific conditions. The extraneous additions of the past that have not withstood the test of time, use and demand have vanished. Whether the innovations of modern times, rubber shoes, beehive hairdoes, nylon shirts and strapless bras – to name a few obvious disasters – will survive these tests, or whether village values change to absorb them as isolation recedes – only time will tell.

a

b

c

e

f

d

g

h

a

b

c

d

e

f

g

h

Japan

a

b

c

d

e

f

g

h

Japan

a

b

c

d

e

f

g

h

i

j

The Towns and the Cities

Caution first: both the romantic's wish that the remote hazy past should be prolonged and the wilful destruction of the past in the name of progress are extremes that should be avoided. The balance is difficult. It is too easy to recognize only the graceful and beautiful in the old crafts and traditions and the vulgar and the coarse in the awkward first steps of modernity. It is important also, not to be blinded to the ignorance and social inequalities of the past, and the potential and inevitability of the future.

The risk of loss is nowhere greater than in Asia. The gap between ancient and modern is wider and more perilous than in the West. The gradual movement from medieval to industrial has been staged over the centuries in Europe. In many areas of Asia, in one brutal stroke populations are thrust from feudal security and archaic systems into the tumult and confusion of the present. Modes of behaviour and traditional dress are the first to be forfeited for half-understood modern mannerisms.

a

b

c

d

b

c

a

d

e

a

b

c

d

e

f

g

h

i

j

k

142

a

b

c

d

e

f

g

h

i

j

k

a

b

c

d

e

f

g

h

a

b

c

d

e

f

g

h

i

j

Uniforms

When the change is violent, the resultant attempts at modern dress and behaviour (and in most contexts modern equals Western, though this is not always true) are at best pathetic, and at worst, neurotic and socially self-defeating. In the unfamiliar ready-made city clothes the uprooting of a farmer forced to abandon his land is even more apparent. The loss of status and identity which dress has always marked has further alienated those with grievances or grudges. Packs of young hoods amble in imitation of the G.I., or with the swagger of the samurai or, with a further loss of identity, with the mincing gait of prostitutes. It would be an exaggeration to find cause in their stridently modern dress, but as an element in the upheaval it adds to the complexity of the dilemma. The generation gap so common in the West is further entangled by a gap of centuries in the East.

Other transitions, without the violence of war or brutal upheaval, provoke thoughts that one cannot escape.

Through my own working involvement with craftsmen and weavers, in villages and in factory towns in India, Hong Kong and Thailand and with an observer's view in Japan, I have seen the village skills giving way to the mechanized uniformity of industrial production. In the back lanes of Srinigar, an old wooden house, a complex of rooms and stone stairways: in a shadowed black-walled room, the air is heavy with brazier smoke. About a dozen men are seated among lengths of woollen cloth. The men with swift sure gestures embroider amid a low incomprehensible mumble of gossip or aimless humming; the heavy fabric lies in great folds and disorder, crowding the small workroom. It is all very dirty and messy. The result, when it is completed and washed, is swirls of soft wool colours, in patterns of incredible ease and beauty. The same view: the folds might be silk or cotton, the skills of another variety, but the general tone, sometimes better or worse, is always the same. Small groups of men or women, children and old bent grandparents, the brazier or teapots in constant bubble. There is a sense of family, of a communal group. There are the sureness and confidence of ability, a sense of accomplishment. There are also squalor and insularity.

These skills that are the basis of a costume tradition are rank with the iniquities of the past and the flowering of a long tradition. A factory producing knitted goods in Hong Kong, a similar site in Bombay: rows of machines matched by rows of people. One views over the hundred heads a well-lit sense of order and organization. A sleeve hem turned with a flashed movement through the machine, and this is repeated until the work bin is full. Another pile of sleeves and the movements are repeated, hour after hour until the day, the month, the year of sleeves is finished. Relatively, the conditions are good, the wages are better than village standards, but one wonders what the total life offers. Coming down from the esoterics of tradition to the small man, the disparities are mixed and the balance is difficult to find.

The benefits of technology and education are apparent in visible terms when one can see the contrast of urban potential and the forgotten medieval towns caught in squalor and hopelessness. As with almost all the advantages of change, set in opposition is the loss of heritage and the safety of traditional expectation. Differences and varieties of dress, as only one aspect of this upheaval, have been levelled to a new and uncertain international style. Yet although on the surface a man in Japan or India may look indistinguishable from all others, deeper in his thoughts and instincts the heritage of the past is still there.

Withstanding the effort, particularly in India and Japan, to revive and strengthen the dress and traditional habits of the past, there is a broader-based movement among the general people towards negation of differences. In self-assured classes the differences are marked with pride, in groups that require the safety of anonymity, the differences are minimized.

Imagine a gathering of small or provincial businessmen, their protective clothing might be shiny suits in gilt-flecked rayon, shoes wedged to upturned toes, glazed Oxford imitations. Their more affluent and sophisticated counterparts are in Cardin suits, Yale collegiate styles or Savile Row innovations, and (depending on what sphere of influence appeals) elegant imported trimmings and fashionable haircuts.

The aristocracy, artists and thinkers, involved with their own sense of identity, often wear the traditional dress, sometimes hybrid concoctions but more frequently the best of traditional apparel. Master craftsmen and the elders of town communities, involved with the traditional skills and habits, are also tenacious upholders of the old costume. The young, who have discovered their own pride and history, though often in a convoluted sense as an imported awareness, have taken the rural dress as a sign of that consciousness.

Among Asian women much more suspicious of change, modesty and more recent considerations of prudery and propriety have confirmed their conservative outlook. Traditional developments and Western clothing are rejected because bright colours are thought of as immodest. Bare arms and legs are considered improper. These are mainly middle-class problems that are the outgrowth of an Asian 'Victorianism'. In Thailand amongst the older generation strict rules of colour and correctness, mostly with the aim of sombre concealment, have forced a garish opposition from the young. In Bangkok during the thirties in an effort to 'civilize' the populace it was a written requirement for women to wear hats, shoes and gloves. Tickets for public transport were not available otherwise. This ruling was fortunately a shortlived one.

In opposition to these timid fears, Asian women have, in large numbers, recognized the advantages of traditional dress. For working women, no other garment combines so many attributes: as carry-all, handkerchief, sun shade and umbrella. When the loose ends are secured, one can imagine no other garment better suited to construction work or heavy field labour. The basic sari, sarong sets and kimono are garments which are difficult to better for work. In their more elegant moods they are undeniably more attractive and more suited to the average Asian build than missionary frocks and the liberated tight sheaths, short skirts or trouser suits. The local fabrics are much more effectively used in uncut lengths or cut in the simple traditional forms as the cheongsam or the kimono. One must also add that the minor dilemma of 'what to wear' is limited to definite choices. Sensible women of modern inclinations are neither slavish to tradition nor constantly opposing it. Fashion, as such, was never a strong element in Asian dress. Stability, rather than change and variety was the strongest urge. Now, as in the West, fashion has become a sometimes wilful but constant revolution. For those who attempt to keep pace, as elsewhere, there is a keenness and the minor satisfaction of being in the stream of things. Massive industries in Asia, mostly in the production of cloth, are based on this satisfaction, so it cannot be regarded as a trivial abbreviation.

Design skills have been misplaced in the multitude of options and other influences. The old talent of fabric and working garments begins to find its way again. The extremes of copying European cuts and cloths and the 'ethnic' cult of pastoral imitations are very slowly synthesizing to a respect for quality and a recognition of a distinctive innovation.

It is obvious that a chemist, pilot or hotelier would not, or should not, wear garments that are best suited for farm labour. It is a fantasy to wish that the dhoti or the body shawl, suitable in their natural and logical habitat, would satisfy the demands, both utilitarian and social, of metiers entrenched in untraditional systems, or that the deep-sleeved kimono is other than a lovely gimmick for the air hostess or lift operator. The Moghul ruler as hotel doorman and the Mongol horsemen as wine waiter are a far (but amusing) cry from first intentions. They are products of the same folksy fallacy that inspires the Austrian shopkeeper to don the bells and ribbons of traditional finery, tempted by tourist expectations.

The options are many, and with the Asian sense of absorption and survival, humour and compromise a direction will come from the present discord. It would be of less importance, this question of old and new, if it were not that within the traditions of clothing and all the crafts of cloth are to be found the fundamental strengths and identities of Asia. The past must give way; one only hopes for replacements equal to the logic and beauty it created.

Notes on the Plates

As costume design remained constant for a long period of time in the Orient accurate dating of costumes is neither necessary nor feasible. Generally it is only possible to ascribe a costume to a certain period or dynasty, which may span several centuries. More precise dates have been given in those cases where they be ascertained, and where the particularities of a costume mark it out.

Front jacket
Noble lady, Rajasthan, 18th century

Back jacket
A samurai and traditional Japanese armour

p. 1   Himalayan lama in procession

p. 4   Cambay noble, India
        Dancer's headdress, Java

p. 5   Shinto priest, Japan

p. 9   Haniwa tomb figure, protohistoric Japan
        Musician wearing a crown-like hat with horns and ears. Though these sculpted figures were funeral decorations, their lively attitudes are far from sombre. As representations of the accumulated wealth and property of the deceased, servants, court figures, soldiers and armour were simply yet accurately portrayed for use and references for the after-life

p. 11   a. Attendant from a pilaster, Śrīraṅgam temple, south India, 16th century
        The figure is dressed in Hindu court style, a short wrapped dhoti heavily girdled with roped jewels, the body is draped with necklaces, circlets and heavy ear ornaments

        b. Chieng San Buddha, late style, Siam, 15th century
        Seated in the Indian or Yogi fashion, the Buddha is in the attitude known as Mara Vijaya, or victory over temptation. In the manner of the later style Chieng San the image is dressed in royal attire (Phra Song Khruang)

c. Shang bronze helmet, protohistoric China, 1600 BC
The Shang helmet was worn with an ornamental feather

d. Nobleman, Nepal, 5th century
A tribal leader in secular style without the trappings of godliness. His hair is in Gupta-style curls

e. Mathura prince, north India, Kushan period, 2nd century AD

f. Head of a queen, Khajurāho, India, 10th–11th century
Both the queen and the Prince (above) are heavily ornamented

g. Indian noble, Greco-Buddhist period (also known as Indo-Greek), 2nd century AD

p. 12   a. Haniwa, female pot-bearer, early Tumulus period, Japan
        This period falls within the half millennium prior to the beginnings of the Buddhist civilization in Japan. This figure is an early extension of the primitive cylinder form in low fire-coiled clay. As so much that remains of early art references depict the aristocracy and the gods, this simple country woman is a refreshing exception. She wears a simple tube-like upper garment and necklace, her hair bun set well back in order to make room for the jar she balances

        b. Haniwa female priestess, Tumulus period, Japan
        This protohistoric shaman wears an elaborate coiffure, two coiled buns resembling the modern Shimada Japanese formal hairdressing style

        c. Terracotta figurine of a goddess, Kulli, India, c 2500–2000 BC

        d. Terracotta figurine of a goddess, Harappa, India, c 2000 BC
        These two mother goddesses are dressed in a style that still exists some four millenniums later (cf. p. 000)

        e. Haniwa warrior in iron armour, protohistoric Japan
        The Kantō warrior wears a torso armour, made of horizontal iron strips riveted together. He wears a helmet and necklace.

        f. Head of a Kusana king, Mathura, India, early first century AD
        The warrior king wears a helmet-like crown

        g. Head of a warrior wearing a studded helmet, Haniwa, Japan

        h. Head of a man, Haniwa, Japan

150

The headdress appears to be a decorative band worn across the forehead, the hair in two braids hanging to the shoulders

i. Head of a boy, Haniwa, Japan

j. Head of a girl, Haniwa, Japan

k. Statuette of a bearded man, Mohenjo-daro, prehistoric India, 2500 BC
The figure wears a headband over a stylized coif, and decorated shawl draped over his left shoulder and an armlet

l. Bronze statuette of a girl, Mohenjo-daro, prehistoric India, 2500 BC
A nude dancing girl with heavy arm bands, her hair is decoratively styled

p. 13 a. Yaksi, Bihar, medieval India, first century BC
This burly attendant carries a ceremonial whisk. Her diaphanous drapery is caught and looped, hanging from a jewelled girdle. She wears heavy anklets and layers of bracelets

b. Ivory statuette of a court entertainer, medieval India, first century AD
Compare her earlier counterpart, p. 12, fig. l

c. Head of a man wearing a crown with bells, Haniwa, protohistoric Japan

d. Head of a man wearing an ornamental headdress, Bharut stupa, India, early Buddhist period

e. Haniwa warrior, protohistoric Japan
Though the proportions are extremely stylized, the warrior stance and manner are highly realistic. He wears a top knot hat; his braids are elaborately twisted. Under his flared coat he wears wide trousers tied at the knees. At his left hand, perched on the flare of his coat, is the archer's wrist protector. A round pommel sword is also worn.

f. Gateway figure, Sanchi, India, end of first century BC

g. Yaksi, Bharhut, India, early Buddhist period
Both ladies wear sparse draperies but with the heavy ankle and wrist ornaments, body jewellery and earplugs

h. Nude torso, Harappa, prehistoric India, 2500 BC

i. Haniwa horse, protohistoric Japan

j. Mother goddess, Patna, India, Mauryan period, 200 BC
The goddess wears an elaborate headdress possibly of flowers, and a deep girdle over an underskirt

p. 14 a. Emperor Lo Ping, China, Ch'in period, 250 BC
The emperor wears a cylindrical headdress with earflaps, a flowing robe with elongated sleeves. The undergarment is girdled just above the waist

b. Shang bronze-footed bowl, China, 16th–15th century BC

c. Harem instructress, China, AD 355
The long gown is stylized as lotus leaves at the hem. Her hair is decorated with jewelled flowers

d. Confucius, China, 551–479 BC
Confucius pictured in the traditional flowing garments of the sage

e. Man riding a horse, tomb figurine, China, Han period, 210 BC
The little soldier on his robust horse wears heavy boot, trousers and a fitted jacket

f. Warrior with standard, Ch'in period, China
The standard-bearer wears the padded garments of the archer warrior

g. T'ang Princess Wen Cheng, China, AD 621–80
The princess wears a silk tippet over her layered robes

h. T'ang lady, tomb figure, China, AD 581
The traditional T'ang gown, cross-closed and waisted high, a long length of fluid drape, her heavy boots scarcely concealed under a pleated undergarment. She modestly wears a cloth draped over her hands. Her headdress rises from a strict coiffure

i. Kneeling official, China, T'ang dynasty
He wears the domed headdress, the mark of his status

p. 15 a. Lady with flute, China, T'ang dynasty

b. Horse in battle saddlery, China, T'ang dynasty

c. Temple guardian, China, 1200
This aggressive warrior god is in padded armour and leg banding. The undergarments are exposed in swirling drapes

d. Kwan Ying, Goddess of Mercy, China, T'ang dynasty
The Buddhist goddess reveals her Indian heritage

e. T'ang lady – rear view of fig. a

f. Sorcerer, China, late Han, AD 550
The Han priest wears a padded torso garment. He wears a lingum on his helmet and has a fierce facial aspect

g. Earthenware tomb figurine, China, Han period, AD 221–580
A folk musician in provincial trousers and shirt, he wears a simple head wrap

h. Tomb guardian, China, Ming dynasty, 1368–1644
The guardian wears layers of quilted armour. His sombre
demeanour is offset by the jewelled symbols of his office

p. 16   Queen Maya and her attendants, Mauryan, India, *c* 300 BC
The visitation of Queen Maya when she dreams of her giving birth
to the Buddha. She is represented here as a Mauryan queen in the
jewelled girdle and hip wrap. Her hair is an enormous coif of
piled braids and jewels. Her maidens-in-waiting are similarly but
more simply clothed

p. 17   Procession, Bagh Caves, India, Gupta period, 4th–5th century
Detail of a wall painting, three women and an elephant mahout.
The country women wear the simple lunghi and choli. The scene in
all its particulars still exists in rural India

p. 20   a. Parvati, Panamalai, south India, 8th century
Detail from a wall mural in the Talagirisvara Temple shows the
goddess in Gupta-style decoration. Her domed crown is a jewelled
structure

b. Head of Bodhisattva, Ajanta, India, early 7th century
The Bodhisattva is portrayed as a Gupta prince in a gold-worked
crown hung with seed pearls

c. Figure in a lotus pool, Jain Cave, Sittanavasal, south India, 850
A young man gathering lotus from a village pool.

d. Weeping woman, Bagh Caves, India, 4th–5th century
All the figures on this page are taken from wall paintings

p. 21   a. Kabuki representation of a samurai lord of the Edo style
Aside from the facial and body painting the costume is Edo style

b. Old woman, China, T'ang dynasty
An old woman in the head covering typical of her stage of life
and the sedate T'ang robe

p. 22   a. Greek warrior

b. Torso of a Greek warrior

c. European horseman

d. Babylonian King

e. His attendant

f. Etruscan matron

g. Babylonian leader

p. 23   a. Bodhisattva, Indo-Greek style, India, 4th–5th century

152

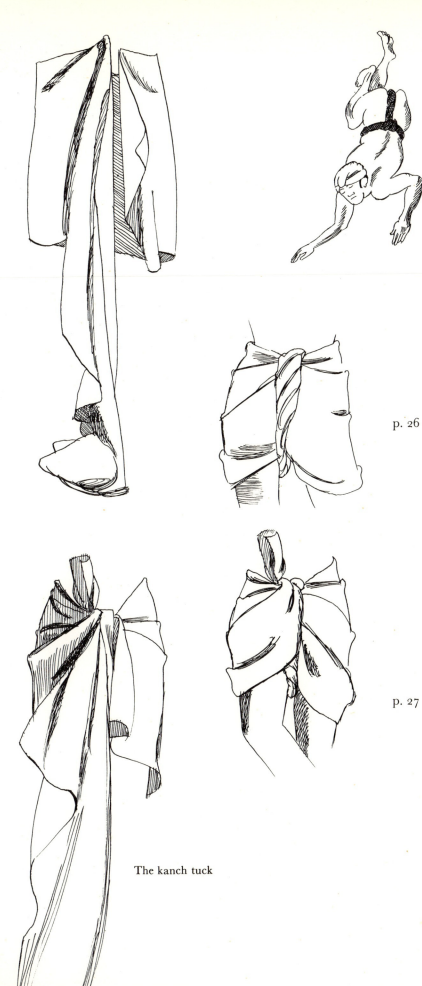

The kanch tuck

A swimmer, Hokusai

b. Dampati couples, Buddhist cave temple, Karli, India, *c* 2nd century AD
Possibly representing courtly donors

c. Woman writing, Khajurāho, India, 10th–11th century
These figures represent the decorated nude

d., e., f. Heads in the Ghandara style, Greco-Buddhist, India

g. Trading vessel, Ajanta, India, early 7th century

h. Gandhara oarsman, Greco-Buddhist, India

i. Goddess, Ceylon, Gupta style, Ceylon, 7th century
The Gupta Empire was heavily to influence her colonies to the south

p. 26   a. Single wrap, short hip wrap, Cambodia, 7th century

b. Single wrap, short hip wrap, Cambodia, Khmer period, 10th–14th century
The stylized drape at the front represents the ends of the wrap draped after tying

c. Single wrap, short hip wrap, Bodhisattva, pre-Angkor, Cambodia

d. Leaf skirt, earliest clothing, Sumeria, 2500 BC

e. Single wrap, short hip wrap, Bonda woman, tribal, India, contemporary

f. Single wrap, long hip wrap, Balinese dancer, contemporary

g. Single wrap, lion-cloth wrap, Saora youth, tribal, India, contemporary

p. 27   a. Double wrap, Central Asia, Afghanistan, 3rd century

b. Double wrap, the shawl with (presumably) a loin-cloth, Bonda man, tribal, India, contemporary

c. Double wrap, the shawl and short hip wrap, Bonda woman, tribal, India, contemporary

d. Extended wrap, the bonze toga, Thai Buddhist priest, Bangkok, contemporary

e. Extended wrap, the Brahmin toga, south India, contemporary

f. Extended wrap, the bonze toga, Thai itinerant priest, Thailand, contemporary

g. Extended wrap, Western Ghat, India, contemporary
The kanch tuck with an extended shoulder wrap

p. 28   a. Extended wrap, Roman toga, Rome, 1st century BC

b. Shawl, the Greek chalmys, classical Greece

c. Dorian peplos, compare p. 29, fig. d

d. Extended wrap, stylized as a sheer wrap, Siam, 6th–11th century
A Torso of Buddha from the Dvaravati period

e. Long single wrap, Chinese Turkestan, 7th–8th century

f. Extended wrap, Chinese Turkestan, 4th century

g. Extended wrap, kneeling priest, Burmese style, late 19th century

h. Single wrap, kanch tuck, Brahmin priest Sukothai, Siam

i. Single wrap, Cambodia, Khmer period, 10th–14th century

p. 29   a. Extended wrap, Laotian priest, Vientian, contemporary

b. Extended wrap, Rajasthan, India, contemporary

c. Extended wrap, the sari, Bengal, contemporary

d. Extended wrap, Rangoon, contemporary

e. Extended wrap, bonze toga, Bangkok, contemporary
Draped arrangement

f. Extended wrap, bonze toga, Bangkok, contemporary
Flat folded arrangement

g. Extended wrap, the sari, female construction workers, India, contemporary

h. Single wrap, the lunghi, Rangoon, contemporary

p. 30   a. Closed sewn garment, Kashmir, contemporary
The pheron worn by men, T-cut with additional seaming at side panels

b. Closed sewn garment, Pakistan, contemporary
The pheron worn by a female construction worker

c. Diagonal closed sewn garment, Mongolia, early 20th century
This garment is lightly padded and bound at the waist. The extended sleeves are folded in a 'hoof' shape

d. Diagonal closed sewn garment, Peking, 20th century
The traditional Chinese robe in coarse cotton

e. Loose open robe worn as an undergarment, Turkey, 1587
A merchant wears the traditional Turkish caftan belted at the waist

The Tibetan cross-closed garment

A ritual dancer,
Sikkim

p. 31 a. Padded loose robe, Caucasus, 19th century
An itinerant trader

b. Turkish caftan, Turkey, 1501
A Turkish painter, after Gentile Ballini

c. Diagonal closed sewn garment, the layered caftan, Mongolia,
19th century
A bridal pair, the groom wears the padded Chinese-style gown
with a padded short sleeveless diagonally closed jacket. The bride
wears the closed sewn robe, buttoned at the centre seam, with a
sleeveless long loose robe. The undergarment has 'horse hoof' cuffs

d. Closed sewn garment, Kashmir, contemporary
The pheron worn by women

p. 32 a. Open sewn garment, China, 7th–9th century
A T'ang tomb figurine of a pedlar. The short jacket is cross-
closed and tied at the waist

b. Open sewn garment, India, 1st century AD
King Kaniska, a feudal war lord of the Mathura kingdom. The
loose quilted coat is worn over a skirt. He wears the heavy felt
boots of a mounted warrior

c. Open sewn garment, Japan, 1185
The Shogun Minamoto Yoritomo. The stiffened over-robe is
double breasted and side closed

d. Open sewn garment, Sikkim, contemporary
Layered over the silk cross-closed silk undergarment is a diagonally
wrapped short jacket and an apron skirt banded at the waist. A
fine silk shawl is draped over the shoulder. Female costume

e. Open sewn costume, Japanese theatrical costume, traditional
Kabuki character

f. Open sewn garment, India, 16th century
The angarkha, the cross-closed Indian fitted robe

g. Open sewn garment, India, 1569
A courtier in the tightly bound robe, waist sashed with a full skirt

h. Loose open robe, Turkey, 1514
Two Turkish merchants, after Dürer

i. Layered open sewn garment, Japanese theatrical costume,
traditional
A Japanese Kabuki character

p. 33 a. Open sewn garment, Korea, 19th century
A Korean nobleman in the layered open robes

Tying the sari

b. Open sewn garment, Japan, 7th-8th century
A sculptor in a working robe, the ends are lifted and tucked into the waist ties

c. Open sewn garment, Japan, Japanese theatrical costume, traditional
The layered cross-closed robes in ritual and dramatic form

d. Open sewn garment, India, 18th century
A wine server, the Coromandel Coast

e. Fitted sheath costume, Burma, 19th century
From a miniature Burmese bronze. The body is bound tightly in draped lengths then sewn and secured after wrapping. Heavily gilt over-garments are worn close to the body

f. Open sewn layered robes, Japan, Heian period, 785-1185
A Fujiwara noble lady in the layered female kimono

g. Open sewn garment, Japan, 7th-8th century
A sculptor in a working kimono, the sleeves are secured at the elbows with separate ties

p. 34   Surya the Sun God, Gwalior, India, Gupta period, AD 320-540

p. 36   a. Noble chieftain, Baroda, 1298

        b. King Krsna, Deva Rāya, south India, 1509-1529

        c. Nepalese deity, 1660

        d. Simhanada, Tanjore

e. Ashoka column, Mauryan period, 269–232 BC

f. Back view of fig. c

g. Symbolic gestures

h. Chandikesvara, Tanjore

i. Benjarahi, Nepal, 3rd century BC

j. God King, Gupta period

p. 37   a. Duleraiji, Jaipur, Rajasthan, 1007–37

b. The King of Oudh, Lucknow, 19th century

c. Emperor Aurangzeb, 1680

d. Emperor Jahangir, 1611

e. Jahangir, 1620

f. The Nawab of Oudh, 1784

g. The Maharajah of Jaipur, coronation robe, 20th century

p. 38   a. Farrukhisiyar, 1750

b. Emperor Akbar, 1590

c. Aurangzeb in his old age, 18th century

d. Bahadur Shah, 1837–58

e. King sitting on the throne, Ahmadnagar, 1565

f. Moghul lord, 1650

p. 39   a. Jahangir as a young man, 1630

b. Akbar, 1605

c. Maharajah of Indore, 19th century

d. Nadir Shah, 1736–47

e. A regal personnage, Jodhpur, 19th century

f. Bahram Gur, a Turkish king

g. The Maharajah of Udaipur, 19th century

h. Babur, 1590

p. 40   The Mandarin dragon, detail from an imperial robe

p. 41   A Manchu noblewoman in winter court robes, early Ch'in
ceremonial dress, 2nd–1st century BC

p. 42   a. A provincial mandarin

b. An emperor, theatrical personification, traditional

c. An empress, theatrical personification, traditional

d. An emperor in summer garment, early Ch'in ceremonial dress,
2nd–1st century BC

e. Kang Hsi, the twelve-symbol imperial robe

f. A Mongolian ruling prince

p. 43   a. Empress with attendants, northern Wei dynasty, AD 522

b. Kang Hsi, the Emperor as a young man, 1654

c. Kang Hsi, the Emperor in middle age

d. Kang Hsi, the Emperor in old age

p. 44   Deccan noble, 17th century

p. 45   Japanese nobleman in traditional regal costume. He is in full court
robe, with wide sleeves and a long train. He wears black lacquered
wooden ceremonial shoes

p. 48   A foresaken, heartsick noble lady, Rajasthan, 18th century

p. 49   The Bodhisattva as a young Gupta prince, Ajanta, 6th century

p. 50   a. Court attendants, Gandhara School, India, 4th–5th century

b. Court dancer, Bali, 18th century

c. Dvaravati musicians, Siam, 6th–11th century

d. Courtier, Siam, Dvaravati period, 6th–11th century

e. Apsaras (temple dancer), India, 16th century

p. 51   a. Court lady, Siam, Chiengsan period, 14th century

b. Court lady, Siam, Dvaravati period, 6th–11th century

c. Palace guard, Siam, Sukotai period, 13th–14th century

d. Lady, Siam, Bangkok period, 1767–1934

e. Dvaravati prince or royal personage, Siam, 6th–11th century

f. Courtier, Siam, Dvaravati period (see p. 50, fig. d)

g. Srivijaya noble, Siam, 8th–13th century

h. Chiengsan male, Siam, 15th–16th century
The figures on this page represent studies by students of the Fine Art Department, Bangkok, from archeological examples

p. 52   a. Apsaras, Khajurāho, 10th–11th century
This sensuous temple dancer represents the voluptuous feminine ideal. She is essentially nude but heavily decorated with body ornaments

b. A royal couple, Ajanta, 6th century
Male and female are equally jewelled

c. Court attendant, mural painting, Ajanta, Gupta period, 4th–6th century

d. Royal consort, south India, reign of King Krsna Deva Rāya, 16th century
The legs are draped in a very sheer length that is gathered and fluted in pleats at the front

e. Khajurāho figure, Madhya pradesh, 10th–11th century

f. Parvati, Ahicchatrā, Gupta period, AD 320–540
Female hair style

g. Siva, Ahicchatrā, Gupta period, AD 320–540
A male hair style

h. Bronze figurine, Korat province, Khmer style, 11th century

p. 53   a. Female deity, Nepal, 15th century

b. Folk couple, Cambodia, 12th century

c. Devout figure, Nepal, 5th century

d. Attendants, Java, 10th century

e. Apsarases (temple dancers) with attendants, mural painting, Sigiriya, Ceylon, 5th century

p. 54   a. Court attendant, Moghul provincial school, 1610–15

b. Court attendant, Moghul provincial school, 1610–15

c. Sheiks in the court of Jahangir, 17th century

d. Moghul pilgrim, reign of Jahangir, 1615

e. Moghul miniature of a child, late 17th century

f. Jahangir courtier, 17th century

g. Moghul courtesan

h. Shah Jahan courtiers, 1650

p. 55   a. Maharatta Peshwa and ministers at Poonah, 19th century

b. Nawab of Cambay

c. H.H. Maharajadhiraja Maharana Bhupal Sing, Rajput, India

d. Governor Elihu Yale, Fort St George, Madras, 1687
The colonial forces maintained their full European costume despite
the pressures of climate. Governor Yale must have suffered in his
wig and layered worsteds and brocades

e. Minister to the Nawab of Oudh, Lucknow, 1784
This portly gentleman is more suitably dressed in sheer layers of
gauze-like cotton. Comfort is a fairly recent innovation in European
dress, but was, despite courtly attitudes that often ran contrary to
this concept, a factor considered in Asian costume

p. 56   a. Noblemen, Udaipur, twentieth century

b. Naik of the Malwa Bhil Corps, 1887

c. Udaipur palace guards, contemporary

d. Maharani of Baroda, 19th century

e. Court lady, Jaipur, 19th century

f. Royal lady, Mewar, 19th century

g. Gaekwar of Baroda, 19th century

p. 57   a. Muslim ladies in full purdah, back view and front view

b. A suppliant at a durbar, Akbar Shah II, 1820

c. Court servant, Moghul Delhi, 19th century

d. Moghul prince at the court of Akbar Shah II, 1820

160

A Haniwa figure

Japanese dowager

Moghul prince

First century god, Madras

e. General Lord Sandhurst, 1857

f. Moghul prince at the court of Akbar Shah II, 1820

g. Moghul prince, Moghul Delhi, 19th century

h. Polo Player, Lahore, contemporary

i. Moghul lady holding a rose, 1775

j. Lord Curzon, viceroy to India, 1908
The viceroy in monumental pose and garb

k. English residents at a tea party, Simla, 1922

p. 58   a. Maharani, India, 1950

b. Muslim lady, northern India, early 20th century

c. Thai court lady, Bangkok, 1900
The beginnings of foreign influence in courtly costume can be seen
here, and in this instance a somewhat absurd combination of
Edwardian and traditional Siamese conventions

d. Wife of an Indian official, New Delhi, contemporary

e. Thai palace guard, Bangkok, contemporary

f. Rajasthan prince at a wedding ceremony, Jaipur, 20th century

g. An Indian official, New Delhi, contemporary
This is a high-ranking official in ceremonial dress

h. A young Thai prince, Bangkok, contemporary
The fitted white jacket and black pah-jungobein are traditional
formal dress

i. Congress-wallah, New Delhi, 1958
An elected official in the white Congress Party 'uniform'. The
attempt to associate power with the aristocracy is in this case
relinquished. The link with the grass roots is stressed with the
wearing of the simple costume of the villages. The attitude of
power is still maintained, however, in this figure

p. 59   a. Thai high-ranking official, Bangkok, contemporary
The ceremonial costume is here totally European

b. Indian high-ranking official, New Delhi, contemporary
The official costume is totally Indian. The 'Ghandi' cap is in fact
the convict's headgear that was adopted as a political statement
against oppressive authority

c. An Indian intellectual, Calcutta, contemporary
The use of simple folk garments in homespun and hand-woven
fibres is a contemporary fashion worn by all classes. When worn
by the moneyed or educated classes it often denotes political or

emotional adherence to values which exclude or defy the innovations from the West

d. Presidential garden party, a high-ranking guest, New Delhi, 1961
The opulence of power gives way to more modest simplicity

e. Young princes, Jaipur, 1950
Remnants of the aristocratic customs, however, are still maintained in formal ceremonies. The young bridegroom and his attendant on the left are typical of this display

f. A Thai royal princess, Bangkok, contemporary

g. Thai suppliants at a royal ceremony, Bangkok, contemporary

h. Prime-Minister Nehru, India, 1947
Nehru possessed great personal elegance. He wore the traditional dress of the aristocrat but with such simplicity that his image was classless and individual

p. 60   A princess of the Chinese court, pre-Mongol conquest, 900

p. 62   a. Kublai Khan, 1260-94
The great Khan in the Mongol woollen robes and fur-lined cap typical of the warrior horsemen

b. Genghis Khan, 1206-27
The fierce aspect of the war lord emperor is heightened by furred headdress, coarse outer robes and sturdy heavy boots. The undergarments of brocaded silks signify his regal calling

c. Kublai Khan, 1260-94
The Khan in ceremonial aspect

d. Mongol courtier, China, 13th century

e. Marco Polo, 1600

f. A Mongol chieftain, China, 13th century

g. Cavalry general, China
This general wears the military apparel of ancient times

h. Hsuan Tsung, Ming dynasty, 15th century

i, j, k. Court ladies and musician, Ming dynasty, 14th century

l. Royal headdress, China, Sung style

m. Mongol chieftain, China, 13th century

p. 63   a. English scholar in Chinese robes, Peking, 1920

b. Manchu lady in formal dress, 19th century
From a stuffed doll, dressed in silk garments

Priest's robe and wrap

Bengal, India

Wrapped garment,
medieval Siam

Mongolian toga

Headgear from Tibet

Medieval Siam

Headdress,
India

Pheron, India

Manchu robe, skirt and hat

Korean cross-closed garment

Closed sewn garment, Kashmir

165

c. Tibetan Lama, Lhassa, contemporary

d. Elderly lady in traditional costume, China, 19th century

e. Upper-class woman, China, 19th century

f. Wife of a Chinese diplomat, Peking, 1925

g. Upper-class city dweller, Peking, 1960
With the effort to break down the class barriers of Chinese society,
this figure is out of step with modern Chinese thought. She
personifies the dwindling old aristocracy

h. An industrialist and his wife, China, contemporary
Despite the drive to equalization, this industrialist pair typifies the
new aristocracy

p. 64   Padded armour of the Japanese war lord, the samurai

p. 65   Traditional armour styles, a samurai in full regalia, a Kabuki
representation

p. 66   a. Noble lady, Kantō region, Japan, 4th century
This Haniwa figure wears a cross-closed tunic over an underskirt

b. Ceremonial spear and battle standard, medieval Japan

c. Young samurai, medieval Japan

d. Prince Shotoku, 574–621

e. Female dancer, Japan, Kamakura period, 1185–1335
The dancer performs the Otokomai, a male dance, in a restrictive
costume with extended sleeves and trousers

f. Court lady, Japan, Heian period, 785–1185
The court costume is worn by a lady of royal family, the Fujiwara

g. Archer, Japan, Heian period, 785–1185

p. 67   a. Samurai warrior, Kabuki representation, traditional

b. Feudal lord, Japan, Ashikaya period, 1530–54
The ceremonial dress of the military classes

c. Korean nobleman, Korea, 1600

d. Samurai hero, medieval Japan

e. Samurai in ceremonial pose, Tokugawa period, 1600

f. Nobleman, Japan, Heian period, 10th century

p. 68   a. High-ranking mandarin in ceremonial court dress
The silk outer garment is decorated with a coat of arms that

166

signifies this mandarin's military status. Officials wear certain insignia denoting rank, though the basic style is the same for all nine grades

b. Hoof sleeve, detail from a woman's ceremonial court dress

c. High-ranking mandarin robe
The breast insignia denotes a civilian official, the gold buttons a seventh rank 'kwan' (mandarin). The sleeves of the undergarment must always conceal the hands. The hat is velvet and rimmed with silk. The crown is of pleated brocade and decorated with ten peacock feathers and long silk ribbons. A gold worked finial tops the crown

d. Ladies' embroidered slippers set on silk covered wooden platforms

e. Sleeveless silk jerkin worn by a woman of rank, northern China
The layered undergarments are in silk, the main robe is lightly padded in silk floss

f. Embroidery detail

p. 69   Fujiwara court lady, Japan, Heian period, 900

p. 70   a. Court attendant, Japan, 18th century

b. Geisha musician, Japan, 19th century

c. Korean noble, Korea, 19th century

d. Court lady, Japan, later Tokugawa period, 1867

e. Hirraga Gennai, Japan, 1728–79

f. Noble lady, Japan, 18th century

g. Royal personage, Japan, 18th century

h. Commodore Perry, 1854
After a portrait by Takagawa Korebumi

p. 71   a. Jesuit convert, Japan, 18th century

b. Council of Elders, Japan, 1841

c., d. A hunting expedition

c. The groom and d. the rider, Kamakura, 13th–14th century

e. Arai Hakuseki, 1656–1725

f. Japanese officers, winter uniforms, 1944

g. Japanese colonel, 1939–45

p. 72   Hindu dress and ornaments, 19th century

Rajasthan

p. 73   Women's quarters, Jaipur, Rajasthan, India

p. 74   a. Village dress and ornaments, Rajasthan, 19th century

b. The nose ring, Pushkar, Rajasthan, contemporary

c. Village woman, Sanganer, Rajasthan, contemporary
The habit of concealing the face to strangers is a remnant of a
stricter system of purdah which demands that women be concealed
to all except for immediate family

d. Village woman, Kashmir, contemporary
Back view of the Muslim purdah over-robe

e. Village woman in full purdah robes, Udaipur, contemporary
Front view

f. Construction worker, New Delhi, contemporary
Her modest gesture of hiding her face seems a curious feminine
contrast to the wiry working gangs of women labouring on
building sites

g. Village woman at a well, Sanganer, Rajasthan, contemporary
The more traditional female chores are almost ritualized in
traditional gestures and movements. Little girls mimic the
movements with an accuracy that has maintained the pattern over
the centuries

h. Woman with baby, Jaipur, contemporary
Curiosity sometimes gets the better of the instinct to conceal

i. The nose ring and jewellery at the hairline, Rajasthan,
contemporary

j. Ladies of the Sultan of Solo's court, Java, 1949

k. Young girl in purdah robes, northern India, contemporary

p. 75   a. Married woman in court robes, Peking, 19th century
Silk tunic layered over a pleated underskirt. Traditional tippet at
the shoulders and hands concealed under the lengthened
undergarment sleeves. Feet are in the lotus shape distorted to
small hooves, known as 'The Golden Lotus'.

b. Detail of the 'lotus' feet in the embroidered slippers and ankle
wraps, China, 19th century

c. Prostitutes, Shanghai, 1870

d. Amah, Hong Kong, 1968
Although the habit of binding the feet has been relinquished, some
older women, victims of the custom, wear little cloth slippers or, in
a particularly grotesque compromise, miniature-sized plimsoles

e. Prostitutes, Shanghai, 1915

f. An upper-class lady, 1920
Her 'Golden lotus' feet are unbound

g. Embroidered slippers, China, 19th century

h. Courtesan, Tientsin, 1915

p. 76 a. Court lady, Japan, 13th–17th century
These extended trousers produced a laboured and mincing gait

b. Village woman, Japan, Kamakura period, 1185–1335
Ladies *en promenade* would conceal their faces under veiled hats

c. Fujiwara courtesan. Heian period, 785–1185
Courtesans were often literate and skilled in poetry and the dance.
This courtesan is dressed as a young prince performing a dance
describing the hero as the 'Overthrower of castles, overthrower of
nations'

d. An unmarried lady out walking, Japan, 19th century

e. Pokkhuri, Japan, 18th century
These wooden clogs concealed tinkling bells in the hollowed
wooden base

f. Black lacquered wooden shoes, Japan, 12th century
Usually worn by men with the ceremonial costume

g. Silk slippers, Japan, 7th–8th century
Worn by noble ladies

h. Fujiwara court lady, Japan, Heian period, 785–1185
A stylized rendition of the twelve multiple layers of robes. The
costume completely dominates the figure so that it seems almost
incidental

p. 77 a., b. Lady at her toilette, Japan, 17th century

c. Courtesan writing poetry, Japan, 1784

d. Lady dressed for going out, Japan, 18th century
A cautious attempt is made here to keep complexions from wind
and sunburn

e. Lady modestly dressed for an evening stroll, Japan, 18th century

f. Lady, Japan, Tokugawa, 1615–1865
With the growth of a wealthy merchant class, artists produced
wood-block engravings that were very popular with fashionable
women and served as 'fashion plates' and guides for hair
arrangements and clothing styles. Intended as fashion illustrations
they attained a high standard of art and poetry

p. 78 a. Suriya, the Sun God, pre-Angkor period, Cambodia

b. Village woman in a religious procession, Bali, contemporary

c. A Mongolian lama in full dress, 1935

d. Brahmin priest, making an offering, Siam, Sukotai style bronze, 13th–14th century

e. Sage with a meditation band, south India, 17th century

f. Priest Ganjin, Japan, Nara period, 7th–8th century

g. Young priest, Wat Mahatat, Bangkok, 1970

p. 79   Head of Yakushi Buddha, Japan, Nara period, 7th–8th century

p. 80   a. Itinerant sage, Punjab, 19th century

b., c. Tantric holy men, contemporary

d. Tantric yogi in procession, contemporary

e. Sri Varsnova Brahmin, south India, contemporary

f. Businessman as a Ganges pilgrim, contemporary

g. Itinerant Sadhu, Rajasthan, contemporary

h. Sikh initiate, Punjab, contemporary

p. 81   a. Young monk in meditation, Bangkok, contemporary

b. Buddhist monk, Bangkok, contemporary
The acolytes are not always slim ascetics . . .

c. Itinerant priest, Chachingsao, 1955
. . . and are sometimes quite jolly, like boyscouts on an outing

d. Buddhist nun, Bangkok, contemporary

e. Morning alms, Bangkok, contemporary

f. Women at temple, Bangkok, contemporary

g. Woman at temple, Rangoon, contemporary

p. 82   a. Shaman headdress, shoes and gloves, N.E.F.A. (North East Frontier Agency), India, 20th century

b. Lord of the Soil, a manifestation of Siva, Kye monastery, Kashmir, 16th century

c. Shaman dancer, N.E.F.A., India, 20th century

d. Shaman, N.E.F.A., India, 20th century
Over the basic caftan the shaman musician wears a jewelled breastplate. His skullcap is fitted with antlers of iron representing a deer. The caftan is decorated with long strips of chamois leather that are tabbed with bells and bits of metal.

e. Skeleton dancer, N.E.F.A., India, contemporary
As fig. a

f. Ritual dancer, Sikkim, contemporary
The robe is of Chinese origin

p. 83   a. A high-ranking lama, Sikkim, 1971

b. Himalayan Buddhist lama, Sikkim, 1969
The small boy is a temple acolyte

c. Lama calling morning prayers, Bhutan, contemporary

d. Lama in procession, Sikkim, contemporary

e. Ceremonial dress, Sikkim, contemporary

f. Ceremonial hat, winter style, Himalayan lama, contemporary

g. Mongolian lama, contemporary
The pleated cloak is in yellow cotton, lined with scarlet satin over a
home-spun cotton robe in saffron. The fur-lined cap with ear flaps
is typical of the Himalayas

h. Mongolian lama, contemporary
This silk-patched toga is worn over rough cotton robes. The
patches of silk sewn in a 'title' formation represent dedication to
poverty and the silk patches are remnants in all tones and shades
of yellow.

p. 84   Peacock dancer, Burma, early 20th century

p. 85   A masked dancer as Ravenna's demon brother, Assam,
contemporary folk theatre

p. 87   a. Krishna as a flute player

b. Siva Natarja, the Cosmic Dance

c. Folk figure of the Lord Krishna as the flute player

d. Siva, as lord of the dance

e. Bronze figure of Krishna as a young child dancing

f. Chanda-li, dancing goddess, Khmer

p. 88   a. Yakshagana actor as Indra, north Kanara, Andhra Pradesh,
India

b. Kathakali head, south India
The elaborate make-up of the Kathakali dancer is painted in
strong primary colours over a thin white coating of rice paste

c. Kathakali dancer as King Jimutavahana, rear view

172

d. Singhalese dancer, Ceylon

e. Masked dancer, Borneo

f. Nijinski as the Blue God (Krishna)
A Russian attempt at Oriental costume

p. 89 a. Barong dancer as a monkey character, Bali

b. Khond dancer as a buffalo, ritual hunting dance, Madhya Pradesh, India

c. Dancer in the role of Krishna as a goatherd, New Delhi

d. Kathak dancer, Rajasthan

e., f. South Indian dancer and drummer, Madras

g. Folk dancer from Tamil Nadhu
Detail of ankle bells and toe ring

p. 90 a. Young dancer, Bali

b. Bharat Nhatyam style, India

c. Bharat Nhatyam style, India

d. Balasaraswati enacting Abhinaya

e. Bharat Nhatyam style, India

f. Veena, instrument from Thajavur

p. 91 a. Folk dancer as Krishna

b. Radha, Kathakali style

c. A Yakshagan, warrior role, Andra Pradesh

d. Radha, Manipuri style

e. Radha, Orissa style

f. Female dancer as male deity, Thai classical dance, Bangkok

p. 92 a. Dancer's headdress, Bastar, Madhya Pradesh

b. Bastar drummer wearing the bison horn headdress Bastar, Madhya Pradesh

c. A young bride, marriage dance of the bison horn Marias of Bastar

d. Khond archer, tribal dancer

e. Khond drummer

f. Bonda female, tribal dance

g. Bonda drummer of the Koraput District, Orissa

p. 93   a. Muslim musician, New Delhi

b. Clown character (Vidushaka), Kudiyattam, Kerala

c. Bharat Nhatyam style, India

d. Actor playing a female role, Ceylon

e. Radha, Kathak style, Rajasthan

f. Kathakali actor in female role

g. Ankiya Nat actor in the costume of a sutradhara (stage manager), Assam

p. 94   a. Young boy dancer, itinerant folk group

b. Thai classical dancer, Bangkok

c. Thai dancer portraying the magical bird (the Garuda), Bangkok

d. Male dancer, Bali

e. Female dancer, Bali

f. Young girl dancer, Bali

g. Young girls being prepared for the dance, Bali

p. 95   a. Thai classical dance, 'The hero Rama conquers the demons', Bangkok

b. Back view of the hero figure, Thai classical dance, Bangkok

c. Burmese classical dancer, Po Sein

d. Garuda, the bird dance, Bangkok

e. Po Sein preparing for a performance, Rangoon

p. 98   a. The dragon dance, at rest, Singapore

b. Chinese actor, the Chinese classical theatre

c. Balinese drummer, Bali

d. Chinese acrobat, Hong Kong

e. Rama mask, demon character, Burma

f. An actor, Srivijaya style, Thailand

g. Masked dancer, Tibet

h. Traditional attitude of the warrior, Chinese classical theatre

p. 99   a. Chinese actor, the Chinese classical theatre

174

b. Bugaku dancer's mask, Japanese Buddhist drama

c. Chinese actress, Chinese classical theatre

d. Chinese actor in the role of emperor

e. Character from a Chinese opera, Shanghai

f. Chinese popular opera, liké, Kowloon, Hong Kong

p.100   a. Kabuki, a samurai character

b. Kabuki, wig styles for male actor playing female roles, front and rear view

c. Noh, the priest Utaura

d. A musician

e. Kabuki, a provincial fool

f. Noh, masked actor as a female, Hagoromo

g. Bunraku Kumagai (Joruri) a puppet's head

p. 101   a. Kabuki actor on stage
The dresser, scarcely visible behind him, is altering his costume for a change in mood

b. Kabuki, 'Wandering through the forest at night'

c. Young boy with a puppet

d. Bunraku doll dance

e. Bugaku, classical court dance

f. Noh, Sagi player

g. Kabuki, a villainous character

p. 102   Banjara gypsy, northern India

p. 104   a. A bridal pair, Vakkaliga, south India

b. Two women, Madras
The women were members of a group of village folk wandering through the halls of Madras Government Museum. Their shaved heads suggest that they were members of a sect of Buddhist nuns.

c. Woman making offering during the snake (Naga) festival, south India

d. Indian astrologer in a market place in Nepal

e. Village woman, near Jaipur, Rajasthan

f. Village children, Madras

g. Village women from Orissa

p. 105   a. Pakistani tea merchant

b. Young boy, Ajmer, Rajasthan

c. Marwari woman in traditional dress and ornaments

d. Tribal girl of the Saoras, south India

e. Young man from Kutch

f. Kashmiri traditional robe and silver ornaments

g. Village man from Saurashtra

h. A young girl with her brother, Assam

p. 106   a. Father and son at a village political gathering, Sanganer

b. Bargaining at a market in Jaipur

c., d., e. Field workers off the main road from Jaipur to Delhi

f. A clerk in Jaipur town

g. Road guard, Rajasthan

h., i., j. Construction workers in Jaipur

p. 107   a. Village woman at Pushkar fair, Rajasthan

b. Small boy in infant's cloak
This would normally be worn by babies as protection from sun and wind

c. Village woman on her way to market, Ajmer

d. Two girls watching a village procession, Sanganer

e. Daughter of a dye master in Sanganer

f. Small child, Sanganer

g. Servant with an upper-class village baby
It is unusual for a villager to be able to afford a servant. This drawing was made in the courtyard of a wealthy fabric printer, featured on p. 109, fig. g

h. Village men at a political rally, Sanganer

i. Young boy on the Jaipur road

j. Boy in a doorway, Sanganer

k. Mother and her children at a village well, Sanganer

p. 108   a. Village girl in her Sunday best, Rajasthan

176

Headgear, jewellery,
Sukothai period, Siam

Tatoo markings,
jewellery, India

Traditional costume and jewellery would not be worn except at fairs, weddings and ceremonies. Her face and arm markings are tattoos

b. Saurashtran woman

c. A tough street worker, Karachi
Women often work on construction sites. They are itinerant city-dwellers, but maintain village dress

d. Prosperous camel dealers, Pushkar fair, Rajasthan

e. Saurashtran man

f. Village woman, Hyderabad

g. Village woman and girl in a market, Ahmadabad

p. 109   a. Two Muslim schoolgirls, Punjab

b. Punjabi festival dress

c. A Bhil woman, Rajasthan

d. Village father and son, Orissa

e. Bengali man, Calcutta

f. Civil servant, Jaipur

g. Master fabric printer, Sanganer

p. 110   a. Ladakhi woman, Jammu, Kashmir
The robe is in a coarse wool with extended sleeves for protection against the cold

b. Woman from the Punjab hills

c. Village woman from N.E.F.A.

d. Kashmiri farmer

e. Saurashtran man in the traditional costume

f. A Muslim fabric merchant, Sanganer

g. A Kashmiri Brahmin woman

h. Palace guard, Agra

p. 111   a. Farmer, Madras

b. Mica gatherer, south India

c. A housewife, Madras

d. Quarry worker, Kerala

e. Young girl, Madras

f. Farmer, Trivandrum

g. Village man, Kerala
A dyer in a printing factory

h. A bazaar merchant, Mangalore

p.112   a. Arm and hand jewellery, Manipuri dancer

b. Silk brocaded jacket, Jaipur

c. Rajasthani woman wearing festive jewellery

d. Face markings and head ornaments, Rajasthan

e. Mirror work and embroidery, an over-blouse

f. Mysore mirror work and embroidery

g. Felt boots, West Bengal

h. Leather shoes, Madhya Pradesh

i. Knitted slipper socks, Jaipur

j. Mirror work and embroidery, Hyderabad, Andhra Pradesh

p. 113   a. b., c. Embroidered tunics and short jacket

d. Lambada woman, Hyderabad, Andhra Pradesh
Her traditional costume is heavily decorated with mirror work and
embroidery. Arms are circled with ivory bangles, and the body
adorned with the silver jewellery of rings, earrings, nose ring and
hair ornaments. Fabric is ornamented with bits of tin, mica, cowrie
shells and glass beads. The whole effect has gained a patina of age
and grime with the mellowing to a fine elegance of what otherwise
would be coarse and garish

p. 114   a. Moghul boot, Moghul king, 17th century
With iron heel, red velvet and gold cloth embroidered in red,
green and gold

b. Man's slipper in appliquéd leather, Raika, Rajasthan

c. Man's leather shoe, stained stripes, Gujar, Rajasthan

d. Man's leather shoe, appliquéd and tooled, Gujar, Rajasthan

e. Man's leather shoe, Ahir, Gujrat

f. Man's leather shoe, Maldhair, Gujrat

g. Woman's shoe sandal in leather, Datia, Madhya Pradesh

h. Kabuli – common leather sandal of rough cowhide

i. Man's straw shoe, Kashmir

j. Village woman, Gujar, Rajasthan early 20th century

p. 115   a. Cabouche – gold fabric with red and gold embroidery, 16th century

b. Woman's leather slipper, embroidered, Jaipur, Rajasthan

c. Bridal sandal of hammered silver, 19th century

d. Modern leather sandal, tooled

e. Woman's shoe in leather, Gujar, Rajasthan

f. Man's slipper, tooled and appliquéd leather, Sathwara, Gujrat

g. Knob sandal of inlaid wood, early 20th century

h. Knitted boot sock, Jaipur, Rajasthan

i. Rajput soldier's shoe and tied leggings

j. Riding boot, 17th century
Iron heeled, red velvet, and trimmed with gold

k. Woman's knob sandal of etched and enamelled metal, 19th century

p. 116   a. Tibetan woman in layered silk robes, traditional
The apron is composed of narrow stiched lengths of striped wool. Her headdress is decorated with coral beads and hung with a black cloth. Her jewellery is inset with turquoise and coral, the necklace of amber beads

b. Large-scale amber and coral beads, a silver neck circlet, Assam

c. An amulet necklace, inlaid turquoise and coral, Lhasa, Tibet
The amber beads are strung on silk threads

d. Rajput warrior with facial painting marking his sect

e. Village woman, Saurashtran
A complex of mixed prints and fabrics

p. 117   a Kabuki actor in make-up, Japan

b. Manchu necklace
A jade circlet hung with amber and coral beads with a silk tassle. The circlet is secured around the neck with braided silk

c. Mongolian boot of appliquéd leather

d. Body painting, south Indian Brahmin

e. Moghul pendant, agate and gold

f. Tippet, detail from a shaman's ritual robe

Cowrie shells are sewn on the cotton base. The edges are hung with iron bells, cowrie and bone

p. 118   a. Muria girl, Bastar

            b. Marias on their way to market

            c. Toda man

            d. Nair woman

            e. Thanda Pulaya, young woman in a sedgebark skirt

            f. Koya woman

p. 119   a. Young man in tribal finery, Saora
                He wears flowers in his elaborate hair-do

            b. Gadaba woman

            c. Malavedam man

            d. Toda bride

            e. Married woman from the Anamalai hills, Kadar

            f. Young woman, Saora

            g. Koya man

            h. Bonda woman

            i. Muria fisherwoman

p. 120   a. Temple ornament, Nepal

            b. Temple staffs, Ladakh

            c. Wooden mask, Sikkim

            d. Ceremonial tippet, Bhutan

            e. Lama, Tibet

p. 121   a. Woman in traditional dress, Sikkim

            b. Assamese woman, Lashai, Mizo Hills, Assam

            c. Young woman, Nepal

            d. Market woman, Bhtan

            e. Winter dress, Sikkim

            f. Village woman, Brahma Putra valley, Assam

            g. Earring and nose ornament, Sikkim

Medieval court dancer,
Siam

p. 122   a. Schoolboy, Bangkok

b. Spinner, Bangkok

c. Villager, Korat

d. Vendor, Bang Phu

e. Boatwoman, Bangkok

f. Fruit vendor in a sampan, Bangkok

g. Man wearing protective amulets and goodluck tattoo, Bangkok

h. Market woman and child, Sampeng market, Bangkok

p. 123   a. Boatman, Bangkok

b. Printer carrying dye, fabric print plant, Bangkok

c. Boy selling lotus pods, Ayudhya

d. Laotian woman in traditional dress, Laos

e. Cambodian woman, Siem Reap

f. Basket seller, Mekong River delta

g. Boat dweller, Bangkok

p. 124   a. Father and son in traditional dress, Burma

b. Woman shopping, Kuala Lumpur

c. Festive processional, Djakarta

d. Construction worker, Malaysia

e. Provincial lady in traditional dress, Thailand, 19th century

f. Provincial lady in traditional dress, Burma, 19th century

g. Court lady, Java

h. Market woman, Cambodia

p. 125   a. Village man, Cambodia

b. Fisherman, Cambodia

c. Temple devotee, Saigon

d. Market women, Saigon

e. Northern Thai villager with leg tattoo, Chieng Rai

f. Temple boys, Laos

g. Silk worker, Thailand

h. Schoolgirl, Bangkok

p. 126   a. E Kaw, young girl, northern Thailand

b. L'wa girl, Ban Pa Pee, Lampoon, Thailand

c. Yao man

d. Karen woman

e. Meo bridegroom

f. Yao girl

g. Meo woman

h. L'wa man

p. 130   a. Peasant couple, China

b. Old woman, southern China

c. Village official, Sze-Chuan province

d. Paddy workers

e. Village woman

f. Woman and child, Hong Kong

g. Boat woman, Hong Kong

h. Boat woman, Hong Kong

p. 131   a. Young men, Sze-Chuan province

b. Seated woman, Changse province

c. Old woman with fan

d. Factory worker, Chungking

e. Villager, Sze-Chuan province

f. Villager, Sze-Chuan province

g. Hong Kong worker at lunch break

h. Hakka woman, Sai Kung, Hong Kong (New Territories)

p. 132   a. Married woman in traditional robes, Mongolia

b. Unmarried woman, Mongolia

c. Mongolian man

d. Mongolian ceremonial robe, Khatkha

e. Wrestler, Ulan Bator, Mongolia

f. Wrestler, Mongolia

182

g., h. Groom and bride, Chahar, Mongolia
The bride is wearing a long sleeveless coat over two layers of caftan

p.133   a. Archer, Ulan Bator, Mongolia

b. Old man, Siberia

c. Village woman, Kouldja

d. Mongolian pilgrim

e. Tibetan horseman

f. Silk sleeveless over-dress, Solouchi, Daghur, Mongolia
The edges are trimmed with embroidered bandings appliquéd to
the dress base

g. Antelope leather shoes, Manchuria

h. Pressed wool boots (felt), Mongolia

i. Woman's slippers, embroidered silk, Mongolia

j. Woman's slipper, embroidered silk, Solouchi, Mongolia
These are the three basic types of shoe of Chinese origin; the flat
sole (i), the raised sole or clog (j) and the turned-up sole (h). The
right and left shoes are identical

k. Leather boot
This soft boot is wrapped and tied around the leg. This boot and
the leather herdsman's shoe (g) are not of Chinese origin but are
typical of the Mongolian nomads

l. Woman and child, Sinking, Outer China

p.134   a. Grandmother and child, 19th century
Ceremonial robe, celebrating the 'Kamioki' (a length of artificial
hair is attached to the child's head in token of a long life)

b. Provincial prince, 17th century

c. Vendor of love letters, the 'Kasoburni-Uri', 16th century

d. Fish pedlar, Iyo Ehime prefecture, contemporary
The kimono is lifted and tucked in the black satin obi revealing
the striped under-kimono

e. Yamagata field worker, contemporary
She wears the 'Kagaboshi', a hood and face protector. Also a
striped work kimono ('Kasuri'), fitted leggings and a cotton apron

f. Straw boots

g. Straw sandals

h. Rice farmer, Toyoma prefecture
Rubber-soled cotton divided slippers are worn over leggings. The
baggy trousers ('mompe') are worn under a back-tied sleeved
apron. Arm-gloves and headscarf are of towelling

p. 135   a. Tsaguru wood gatherer, Japan
For cold and rainy weather, the wearer is protected by a straw
cloak (kera), velvet arm-gloves, wrapped leggings (hoshi) and straw
shoes that are worn with snow shoes

b. Rice planter, Kochi
The cotton ikat kimono is tied up at the waist with the underskirt.
The full sleeves are tied with a cotton banding that criss-crosses
the back. The head is wrapped in towelling

c. Female field worker, Yamagata prefecture
The face mask (Henkotana) is tied over the headscarf (Furoshiki).
The working costume is composed of layered cotton kimono,
apron and hakama trousers

d. Rice planter, Himi
The rush hat is worn over a cotton headwrap

e. Shop keeper, Kyoto

f. Yamagata field worker
Wearing the striped work kimono (Kasuri), face mask and head
wrap

g. Yamagata field worker (back view) as fig. c

h. A farmer's wife

p. 136   a. Traditional bridal costume

b. Small girl in ceremonial dress

c. Japanese pilgrim

d. Aikawa woman

e. Japanese priest

f. Rural construction worker

g. Fisherman

h. Geisha

i. Sumo wrestler

j. Fisherman

Figure of Radha, Rajasthan, 1735-88

p. 137   Married woman, Khalkha tribe, Outer Mongolia
The robe is made of Chinese silk bought from itinerant Chinese merchants. As the fabric is precious and in short supply it is often patched of several patterns and worn on ceremonial occasions for a lifetime. The robes are consequently glazed with oil and the stains of long usage. The raised sleeves and horse hoof cuffs are typical of the area. The velvet cylinder hat is worn jauntily. The headdress is stiffened horsehair. A length of false braid is attached. Silver chains and beads are hung from the temples. A sleeveless jerkin is cross-closed in Chinese fashion

p. 138   Street scene, Hong Kong

p. 139   a. Young Indian couple, Janpath, New Delhi, 1971

b. Young man, Bangkok

c. Beauty queen aspirant, Bangkok

d. Shop assistant, Bangkok

e. Young girl, Petburi Extension, Bangkok

f. Student, Tokyo

g. Japanese couple, 1965

h. Marching students, Shanghai

p. 140   a. Classical dancer being prepared for a performance, Bangkok, 1960

b. Woman shopping, Bangkok

c. Market woman, Bangkok

d. Traffic policeman on duty, Bangkok

p. 141   a. Traffic policeman on duty, Hong Kong

b. Woman shopping, Hong Kong

c. Market woman and child, Hong Kong

d. Office worker, Hong Kong, 1965

e. Prostitute, Bombay

p. 142   a. Part-time merchant, Soi Sai Nam Phung, Bangkok

b. Little girl, Hong Kong

c. Father and sons, China

d. Schoolgirl, Harding Bridge Road, New Delhi

186

e. Visitor at the Tokyo Zoo, Japan, 1968
Japanese children are dressed with care and pride for special occasions

f. Four-year-old girl helping with household chores, Bangkok
Children's clothes are often inventively functional

g. Big brother and little brother, Hong Kong
Elder children care for their younger brothers and sisters

h. Eight-year-old young lady, Bangkok

i. Chinese amah (servant) with her charge, dock area, Bangkok

j. Village schoolgirl, Sanganer, India

k. Sikh schoolboy, New Delhi
Sikh young boys wear crisp handkerchiefs at their top knots

p. 143   a. Dock worker, Bangkok

b. Factory workers, China

c. Factory worker, Tokyo

d. Electrician, Punjab, India

e. City office worker, China, Canton

f. Factory worker, China

g. Political student, China

h. Street vendor, China

i. Army officer, China

j. Riot police, Tokyo

k. Labourers, Punjab, India

p. 144   a. Tokyo businessman, 1964

b. Office worker, Bangkok, 1971

c. Housewives on a bus, Tokyo, 1968

d. Tokyo students, 1968

e. Winter dress, Tokyo, 1968

f. Painter, Tokyo gallery, 1968

g. Seamstress, Bangkok, 1969

h. Showgirl off duty, Bangkok, 1971

p. 145   a. Delhi office worker, winter dress, India

b. Cricketer, New Delhi

c. Clerk, Bombay

d. Businessman, India

e. Designers, on the road to Jaipur, India

f., g., h. Entertainers, Bangkok

i. Model, New Delhi

j. Hotelier, New Delhi

p. 146   a. Chinese envoy in London

b. Pakistani negotiator

c. Grand Palace sentry, Bangkok

d. Thai soldier, Bangkok

e. Construction workers, Tokyo underground

f. Chinese factory worker

g. Peking demonstrators

h. North Korean official

i. Post Office worker, Bangkok

p. 147   a. Bangkok student

b. Traffic Police, Madras

c., e. Tokyo students

d. Thai student, Bangkok

f. Universal fashion, Tokyo model

g. Government guard, Chandigarh, India

h. Young student, Tokyo

189

Geisha girl

Some Common Terms

achkan: fitted coat, the length is usually cut just above the knee (India)

angarkha: cross-closed fitted robe (India). The closure design is either diagonally crossed or in circular shape with a bib-shaped underpiece

aoidai: female dress (Vietnam). A long fitted sheath is slit to the waist at the side seams and worn over long trousers. It is a variant of the Chinese choengsam

burka: Muslim veil or long purdah robe which conceals the face and body

caftan: loose robe with long sleeves. It is open at the front and often girdled at the waist.

chadar: Indian or Persian shawl

chalwar: Turkish pantaloons; Indian baggy trousers

chiton: rectangle of cloth secured to the shoulders and girdled at the waist (classical Greece)

chlamys: classical Greek military cloak

choengsam: woman's sheath-like costume (southern China)

choli: short bodice, cut just below or halfway across the bust leaving the midriff bare, or alternatively cut just to the waist level

chupa: full-cut robe with high collar (Tibet). It overlaps at the front and is tightly bound at the waist

dhoti: hip wrap as divided 'trousers' (India, South-East Asia)

dragon robe: imperial court dress (China)

furoshiki: square cotton cloth used as a headscarf or wrap for carrying small objects (Japan)

gandoura: woman's caftan including head covering (India)

geta: wooden clogs (Japan)

gharara: loose trousers, full cut and gathered as a divided skirt (India)

hakama: tight-legged trousers (Japan)

hankotana: face mask (Japan)

himation: a large rectangle of cloth (6 ft by 9 ft) often worn as a wrapped undergarment under a cloak, or as an outer garment (classical Greece)

hōshi: leggings (Japan)

ikat: tie die cloth. The weft, and occasionally warp and filler threads, is pre-dyed to form a woven pattern

jama: Moghul coat (India) ('pyjama' is an English derivative)

jamewar: mantle or coat (India)

kaga bōshi: cloth hood wrap (Japan)

kamis: overshirt or undergarment (India)

kamishimo: man's overgarment (Japan)

kanch tuck: the divided 'trouser' wrap. A tail of cloth is twisted and tucked into the small of the back

kasuri: striped cotton work kimono (Japan)

kera: straw cloak (Japan)

kimono: cross-closed open-sewn garment (Japan). As an outer garment it is worn by both men and women

kurta: man's shirt (India). A loose-cut long shirt, the hem length hangs longer at the side slits and the sleeves are often set at right angles to the body cut. The neck is round and collarless or is set with a narrow raised collar. Its closure is usually buttoned with studs

lunghi: man's hip wrap as a long or knee-length skirt (India, South-East Asia)

mompe: baggy trousers (Japan)

muna-maedare: apron (Japan)

obi: woman's waist wrap (Japan)

pah-jungobein: hip wrap as divided 'trouser' (South-East Asia – Thailand, Cambodia)

palu: decorative cross border at the end of the sari length (India)

pari dhāna-vasana: lower garment tied with belt or string (ancient India)

passin: hip wrap cloth (sarong) (South-East Asia)

pheron: Kashmiri robe or shirt, closed sewn garment (India)

pokkuri: thick soled clogs (Japan)

prāvarā: cloak or mantle (ancient India)

sari: female body cloth, wrapped garment (India)

sarong: female body cloth, wrapped garment (S.E. Asia)

shitatare: sleeveless garment cut to and wrapped at the waist (Japan)

sode-nashi: sleeveless jacket (Japan)

tabi: toed sock worn with geta or zori, or alone as indoor footgear (Japan)

uttariya: upper garment (ancient India)

zori: thong-toed sandal (Japan)